Naming the Child

Hope-filled Reflections on Miscarriage, Stillbirth, and Infant Death

Jenny Schroedel

PARACLETE PRESS
BREWSTER, MASSACHUSETTS

Naming the Child: Hope-filled Reflections on Miscarriage, Stillbirth, and Infant Death

2009 First Printing

Copyright © 2009 by Jenny Schroedel

ISBN: 978-1-55725-585-3

All Scripture citations are taken from *The Holy Bible, English Standard Version*®, Copyright © 2001 by Crossway Bibles, a division of Good News Publishers. All rights reserved.

Library of Congress Cataloging-in-Publication Data
Schroedel, Jenny.
 Naming the child : hope-filled reflections on miscarriage, stillbirth, and infant death / Jenny Schroedel.
     p. cm.
 ISBN 978-1-55725-585-3
 1. Consolation. 2. Miscarriage—Religious aspects—Christianity.
 3. Premature infants—Death—Religious aspects—Christianity. 4.
 Infants—Death. I. Title. BV4907.S43 2009
  248.8'66--dc22
                                     2008045548
 10 9 8 7 6 5 4 3 2 1

Published by Paraclete Press
Brewster, Massachusetts
www.paracletepress.com
Printed in the United States of America

For
Garrison

Contents

Introduction

*L*ast summer, when I was round with my second child, perpetually devouring ice cubes as Natalie somersaulted in my womb, a friend came to visit. I knew from mutual friends that she'd recently had a miscarriage, but she hadn't yet told me herself. And I was afraid—in the way that everyone seems to be—of what I would say and how I would say it. I hoped that I could somehow be present to her, that my expanding belly would not create a chasm between us.

As I drove to the airport, I wondered how she might bring it up, or if I should, and if I did, how I would. Despite my healthy pregnancy, the shadow of grief hung over that year—we'd lost three friends in eight months, all under the age of thirty. In our tiny parish, five women conceived and announced their pregnancies, but only three brought the babies to term. Death was all around us, and yet I found myself tongue-tied when Jenny climbed into the car beside me.

After telling me a little bit about her flight, she mentioned the miscarriage, and then she said something I'll never forget. She said, "After my miscarriage, I realized that I needed to tell my story in the same way that other women need to tell the stories of their labors."

This book grows from three needs: the need to tell, the need to hear, and the need to understand. The desire to write it grew organically from my own life. Although I have not experienced a miscarriage or the death of my own infant, my oldest brother, Garrison, died shortly after he was born. His death colored my childhood in all sorts of ways I could not articulate or understand.

As an adult, many of my friends have experienced miscarriage, stillbirth, or the death of an infant within the first months of life. Their stories often surprise me because they are not just heartbreaking. They are also love stories in the purest sense—stories of agony and hope, anguish and expectation. As I heard more and more over the last several years, I longed to weave them together into something cohesive so that bereaved parents would feel less alone.

These parents helped me to better understand that raw spot in my own family history, a place that was still awaiting redemption. My brother Garrison was born in the early 1970s with a severe case of spina bifida. After he was born, my parents were told by their doctors to leave him in the hospital to die. Overwhelmed with shock and grief, they did as they were told.

While Garrison was still alive in the hospital, the pastor kept asking how he could help. "Could I buy groceries for you?" he asked. "Any errands I could run?" Again and again, they told him these things weren't necessary. But one day he showed up on their doorstep with an offer they could not refuse.

"May I baptize your son?" he asked. So Pastor Carroll went alone to the hospital, sprinkling the swaddled and dying Garrison with the waters of life. Over the years, I've tried to recreate this scene in my mind. I know so little about what really happened, but I like to imagine that Garrison looked up at Pastor Carroll with bright and waiting eyes, that he recognized this love for what it was and took it with him when he left.

I don't think my parents' story is unusual for their time—Garrison was born at a time when many felt that it was better for parents not to bond with their dying infants. It was considered just too painful. Dying or dead infants were often whisked away by hospital staff in an effort to "protect" the parents from the full implications of what had happened. But this type of protection always backfires. Instead of having an outlet for their grief, parents bear it in silence. Their bodies, which have spent a lifetime gearing up for the tasks of bearing children and raising them, do not easily forget.

As I spoke to more and more parents, I was glad to hear that most who experienced stillbirth or gave birth to a terminal baby were given the opportunity to hold and bond with their child. Many experienced compassionate care from hospital staff. Still, experiences vary, and this is especially the case with miscarriages. Many wished there had been more support through religious rituals or counseling. And with every story I heard, I became more aware of the variables—you just don't know exactly what might happen to you or how you might respond. The death of an infant requires parents to make a series of difficult decisions when they are least equipped to make them, which is another reason I wrote this book. I want parents facing end-of-life decisions about their infants to know that they have choices, and that their instincts are a valuable tool as they navigate this uncharted terrain.

Each chapter has two sections—one devoted to story and reflection and the other to practical information about what you or someone you love can do after the death of an infant or in preparation for it.

The Forbidden Room

One night while I was working on this book, I had a strange dream. I dreamed that I had a room in my house I had never found before. Nobody had told me where it was or that it existed, and I just kind of stumbled inside.

The room was full of all sorts of memorabilia I'd never seen, including Garrison's death certificate, his footprints and fingerprints, and a manila envelope with photos. There was a man outside of the room who urged me not to go in. When I picked up the envelope he shook his head violently. "Do not look at those," he said.

But I couldn't resist, not after a lifetime of wondering. So I opened the photos and finally saw what he looked like, the brother I have wondered about all my life. He didn't look at all well, but he was undeniably recognizable as my own brother. The dream only reinforced a reality that I encountered time and time again while I worked on this book: death remains a taboo subject, and there is none more taboo than that of an infant.

Infant death is a forbidden room. We don't want to speak about it or engage with it or be open to the questions it stirs up. When I told people that I was writing this book, they would take a step back. "Why," they would ask, "would you want to write about that?" But their initial resistance would almost always give way to an admission such as, "That happened to my sister," or, "That happened to my mother," or, "That happened to me."

Despite broader cultural resistance, bereaved parents invited me into their own forbidden rooms. They've learned over the years to keep the door open, at least a crack, because it is only by entering that room that they are able to remain connected to the children that they never stop loving, never stop dreaming of and aching for.

So I invite you to enter this room with us. Once inside, you'll find that it is not as frightening as you might have imagined. It's a human place, full of stories and laughter and tears. And every story has a stroke of unexpected grace: each contains an unmistakable connection to life.

Ultimately, these stories are not just about death, but about life—about how we live and love our children and care for them as they die, and beyond. These are also stories of transformation. As Igor Kostin, the first photographer at the Chernobyl nuclear accident in 1986 said, "It's hard to live among normal people now. A person who has been through hell has a different attitude. He breathes the air and feels the sunshine differently."

Many of these parents—who will never breathe the air or feel the sunshine in the way they once did—spoke of the surreal experience of climbing into their cars in the hospital parking lot and driving away from their dead or dying infants. For those who had to leave a baby behind, I hope this book will also create a way to bring your child home—if not from the hospital, at least into hearts and families and friendships. We make room in the home of our hearts by sharing the stories of our children, by practicing random acts of kindness in their honor, and by saying their names again and again, even as we open our arms to let them go.

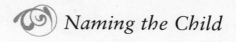 *Naming the Child*

Nobody knew you
"Sorry about the miscarriage dear, but you couldn't
have been very far along."
. . . existed.
Nobody knew you
"It's not as though you lost an actual person."
. . . were real.
Nobody knew you
"Well it probably wasn't a viable fetus. It's all for the
best."
. . . were perfect.
Nobody knew you
"You can always have another!"
. . . were unique.
Nobody knew you
"You already have a beautiful child. Be happy!"
. . . were loved for yourself.
Nobody knew you
. . . but us
And we will always remember
. . . You.

—*"Nobody Knew You"* by JAN COSBY

*I*n the streets of Japan, you probably won't hear Japanese equivalents for terms like *fetus* or *product of a pregnancy* to describe the unborn. Instead you'll hear a gentler term, *mizuko*, which literally means "a child of the waters." This term is also used for miscarried babies, aborted babies, stillborns, or those who died shortly after birth, to express the Japanese belief that human life emerges slowly, progressively, in the warm waters of the womb. Babies who never have the opportunity to breathe our air return to the liquid state from which they came. The *mizuko* are not of this world—they barely entered it, after all—but they retain a cherished place in families and communities.

There are shrines in temples and homes for the *mizuko*, called Jizo shrines, with statues of babies. Mothers sew red caps and aprons for the statues, tucking notes with messages like, "Forgive me," or, "I will never forget you," into the aprons. They adorn the statues with colorful pinwheels, returning again and again with other siblings and the father to leave toys and other gifts for their water baby.

These shrines are not the bleak, tearful places you might imagine—some are even located in parks dedicated to the *mizuko*, with swings and slides for siblings to play on while their parents visit the shrine. Imagine peals of laughter as the older kids run about, while the parents bow before their shrine, lighting a candle or stick of incense.

There is something so refreshingly everyday about the Jizo shrines—so fitting for the ever-present nature of the parents' grief. The oldest Jizo shrines can be spotted on roadsides and street corners. Here, women take turns washing the shrine, adorning it with flowers, and leaving food. These shrines call communities to a continual remembrance. As people go about their daily business, they can't help but see the shrines, and all that they represent.

After talking to many women who experienced miscarriages, I'm struck by the contrast between the American and Japanese experience. In Japan, this grief is not hidden out of sight. It is not borne exclusively by the mother, but also by siblings, by extended family, by entire communities. And in Japan, the grief and love have a tangible outlet—there is something to do: a hat and apron to sew, letters to write, a pinwheel to purchase, a place for the other kids to play. Like housekeeping, the work goes on. The shrine must be cleaned, there are flowers to pick and arrange, and new clothes to sew as the seasons shift.

Naming the Child

In contrast to the Japanese, those in the Western world don't have much to say about babies who die in the womb, especially when the death is early. People wrongly assume that if there is no body to bury, there will be no grief. Most do not understand how quickly parents can become attached to their babies in utero. Miscarriages do not just mark the end of a few weeks or months of pregnancy. Pregnancy is not just about the present and future—it is also about the past. For some, the tiniest zygote represents a lifetime of longing for a specific and irreplaceable child.

In most hospitals, tiny, unnamed fetuses are discarded as "medical waste." Mothers are rarely offered counseling or religious services. They are expected to get back on their feet as quickly as possible. There is barely time to heal physically, let alone emotionally. There is no sanctioned time of grief, no accepted etiquette as to how one might help or support those most directly affected.

Like the Japanese who have found a way to connect with their unborn babies, others need a way to make the death of the unborn concrete—and a way to continue to remain connected to their offspring as the years wear on. Some women won't want to knit caps or create shrines for their babies, but there is something that can be done—something intuitively human and spiritually permanent.

You can begin by naming your baby.

Reach toward a name that acknowledges the unique and precious person that was taking shape in the quiet darkness of the womb, a name that bears the hope and anguish you associate with this child.

There are no rules for naming—it doesn't really matter if you knew the sex, or if you held or saw him or her. It is enough if you loved the child—even if you didn't consciously love him or her at the time, but realized later—sometimes even years later—that you ache for him or her.

From a Judeo-Christian perspective, naming is a holy act. In the very beginning of the world, God names the darkness and light, the sky and the sea. Isaiah 49:1 even suggests that God names the unborn: "The Lord called me from the womb, from the body of my mother he named my name."

Perhaps naming is so natural and necessary because it is the first task mentioned in Genesis. Long before Adam was warned about the Tree or punished for his disobedience, he was asked to call out names for all the animals. Whatever he said, stuck. And even before the first human being was created, God named the night and day, the darkness and the light.

In naming, we have a chance to be like God, to speak the name that will open the door to the reality of what has happened and who our baby is. Perhaps naming the baby is the most transcendent act available to us. Long after mementos from the pregnancy or birth are put away, long after the insanity and intensity that marks the first year of grief, the baby still has a name, and we can still speak it.

Connecting with Your Baby

To speak the baby's name is to move the child from the abstract into the concrete. No woman has ever borne a generic child. Every being that begins to form is unique and precious. This truth is something that most parents know instinctively, but others are not always so quick to catch on. When you publicly speak the name of your baby, you're no longer talking about "pregnancy loss" or "infant loss" but about an unrepeatable human being that had already begun to have a relationship with his or her parents and siblings, even in the womb.

Sometimes we don't have a chance to see or hold our babies, but it is unfair to say that these children are unknown. Many pregnant women begin to "know" their babies long before quickening, in all sorts of subtle and not so subtle ways. When I think back on my two pregnancies, I remember a sense—almost overwhelming, at times—of the particular, unique child I was bearing. While I could not articulate anything about my children's looks or temperaments, I had an intuitive sense of what it was like to "be with" each child, a sense that was confirmed later as I watched them grow into life.

In her book *Expecting Adam*, Martha Beck describes a similar phenomenon during her pregnancy: "I had the same feeling about my son, already, that I had about anyone else I deeply loved. I knew him. I felt him, the way you feel a loved one's presence when you are together, even when no words are spoken. . . . I had an almost tangible sense of my son's personality, his unique and indestructible identity. The idea of losing him was simply unthinkable."

Perhaps the encounter that begins in pregnancy is not unlike the encounter we might have with a person when they are near death, even when they can no longer speak or move or see. Some people say that those with Alzheimer's are "no longer there," but my own experience with my husband's grandmother testifies to something else. Even after Sally lost the ability to articulate herself and navigate the concrete details of life, she was still Sally, perhaps more Sally then she had been in her healthiest state. Something about her utter helplessness and dependency near the end brought her essence to the surface—it was right there, available to anyone who could open the eyes of his or her heart.

Discerning the Name

Cultures around the world and most major religions have naming rituals that mark a critical threshold for a newborn baby. In my own tradition as an Eastern Orthodox Christian, a child is named on the eighth day, because that day completes the cycle of the world's first week.

Naming is customarily done after birth, but when a death occurs in the womb, the resulting grief and chaos can undo what might have been an orderly process: conception, pregnancy, birth, naming. Against this chaotic backdrop, naming the child is all the more important, and can bring some solace and help to parents who wish to forge an eternal bond with the child they did not get to know.

Parents discern a name in many different ways. Sometimes it comes to them in a dream. Before I begin to tell my friend Juliana's story, I need to say something: she hates the term "miscarriage." She feels that it minimizes the grief associated with the tiniest of babies, and that it suggests that the woman did something wrong: had she "carried" the baby better, he or she would still be alive. I use this term in this and other stories for lack of a better word, simply because it will be recognizable to all.

Just near the end of the first trimester of her pregnancy and just before her miscarriage, Juliana had a dream that revealed her son's name. Juliana had just seen him for the first time, through an ultrasound. In the ultrasound, he was perfect, with tiny arms and legs. Then, just before he left her body, she had a dream that cast him into the future: "A day or two before he died, I dreamed of a chubby blond toddler who was running away from me. I kept chasing him and finally caught him. When I asked what his name was, he said, 'My name is Philip.'"

Juliana's miscarriage began with bleeding and cramping, and then Juliana went to the bathroom and delivered him into her hand. As her husband, Stephanos, held him, she announced, "His name is Philip."

For Juliana, the process of naming was not so much about "coming up with the right name," but more about finding the way to the name that already belonged to her son. She believes that God first names the child and then it is the spiritual work of the parents to find their way to the name.

Many who experience miscarriage feel that naming the baby doesn't just help them personally, but it also helps others to understand that while the baby may have been tiny, the ache is often enormous. For Juliana, naming her son marked a threshold. "It was helpful for us in the grieving process to have named Philip, rather than just talking about 'the son we lost,'" Juliana explained. "It helped us to carry his soul with us and to keep his memory in a concrete way. Now I can say, 'My son, Philip.'"

My friend Dennise Kraus, after one ectopic pregnancy and one miscarriage, said something similar: "Naming an unborn child is a powerful thing. It is a way to acknowledge to the world what God already knows. A way to say, 'life is precious—this life is precious.'"

For Dennise, the names of her children just kept coming back to her, rising up inside until she could not resist them. And after she named her babies Rachel and Gabriel, people related differently to her experience. Dennise is the wife of an Orthodox priest. Each year when her church commemorates the day that the angel Gabriel came to Mary to tell her she would bear a child, hearing the name "Gabriel" sends shivers up Dennise's spine.

Something to Do

Many of the mothers I spoke with found out mid-pregnancy that something was wrong with the baby. With this devastating knowledge, the act of naming the baby sometimes became the one hopeful, constructive act available to them.

Rachelle Mee-Chapman selected a name for her son when she discovered, in the fifth month of her pregnancy, that her son was terminal. During a routine ultrasound she found out that he had missing vertebrae, no chest or abdominal wall, and a malformed heart. In the midst of her and her husband's incredible shock and grief, naming their son was one constructive and tangible way to respond.

There was only one week between their son's diagnosis and the induced labor. Rachelle and her husband had already decided to try to give their son a name that would be reflective of both his family heritage and his spiritual heritage. Raised Lutheran, Rachelle had grown up singing the song of Simeon:

> *Lord, now you are letting your servant depart in peace,*
> *according to your word;*
> *for my eyes have seen your salvation*
> *that you have prepared in the presence of all peoples,*
> *a light for revelation to the Gentiles,*
> *and for glory to your people Israel. (Lk. 2:29–32)*

Rachelle was comforted by the promises she saw in Simeon's experience—he had seen the salvation of God and had gone to rest in his arms. "I wanted to name that truth for my child as well," she says.

But Rachelle and Paul also wanted a name that would reflect their family heritage, and they came to one that had both the family and spiritual dimensions they wanted. Rachelle and Paul were in graduate school when she became pregnant. Their professor,

Eugene Peterson, liked to quip that if Prozac had existed in King David's time, the essential rage and grief of the Psalms would have been lost. He believes that rage is part of the fabric of life and God prefers it to indifference. So Rachelle and Paul decided to give Simeon a middle name that allowed them to express every emotion they experienced surrounding their son's death—in the light of this reasoning, they named their son Simeon David.

Speaking the Name

This past year, on October 15, Father Martin and Dennise Kraus held a service at their parish for miscarried babies. October is National Pregnancy Loss Month, and October 15 is Pregnancy Loss Awareness Day. On that day, all over the country, parents who have experienced a miscarriage, or have known someone who did, light a candle for that child.

Just a few people attended the service the Krauses held, during which they wrote down the names of these babies and prayed for them. During the service, Dennise said she and the others in attendance kept going back to the list to write names again and again as they remembered more and more babies that had died in the womb. She was astonished at how many women she knew who had experienced miscarriage.

There was one baby that hadn't yet been named. So on that list of names, one woman wrote, "The baby whose name is known only to God," and that was just how Father Martin prayed for the baby when he came to that spot on the list.

After C.S. Lewis's wife died of cancer, his friends did not know what to do with him. He wrote in his journal, which was eventually published as *A Grief Observed*:

> *An odd by-product of my loss is that I'm aware of being an embarrassment to everyone I meet. At work, at the club, in the street, I see people as they approach me trying to make up their minds whether they'll "say something about it" or not. I hate it if they do, and if they don't. Some funk it altogether. R. has been avoiding me for a week. I like best the well-brought-up young men, almost boys, who walk up to me as if I were a dentist, turn very red, get it over and then edge away to the bar as quickly as they decently can. Perhaps the bereaved ought to be isolated in special settlements like lepers.*

Lewis's experience is certainly common among parents who experience infant death, especially those who have miscarriages. People don't know what to say; often, to avoid the shame of saying something wrong, they say nothing at all.

For those who experience the death of a baby in the first year, their baby's name can also become strangely taboo. Friends and family might hesitate before mentioning the name, fearing it will bring too many emotions to the surface. But for bereaved parents, speaking the child's name is part of their healing.

Bereaved parents and siblings need to feel free to say the name of their child, to share their memories of the pregnancy or of the child's short life. They think about that child often, anyway. It is helpful to be able to speak about him or her, too. There are many concrete ways to keep a baby's name alive, such as including the name on holiday cards, mentioning it in e-mails, or having it engraved on a bracelet for the mother to wear.

Dr. Joanne Cacciatore, whose daughter Cheyenne died during labor, developed "The Kindness Project," yet another way of honoring a baby's name and existence. The project was birthed out of her own need. That first year after Cheyenne's death, Joanne dreaded Christmas. The only way she felt she could get through it would be to do something in Cheyenne's honor. So Joanne calculated all the money she would have spent on Cheyenne, had she lived, during her first months and at Christmas, and she used this money to buy eight girl presents and six boy presents.

On Christmas Eve she went to a hospital in Phoenix, hoping to distribute the gifts to children who had to spend Christmas there. When she checked in she discovered there were no children there. As she turned to go, the receptionist told her to go to the Head Start Program down the street, which provided care for low-income parents, many of whom had to work on Christmas Eve.

The center director was thrilled when Joanne walked in with Santa's sack because many of the children would not be receiving any gifts that year. And then

Joanne discovered that there were six boys and eight girls there that night—exactly the amount of presents she had purchased!

As the months wore on, Joanne continued to be inspired to do random acts of kindness in Cheyenne's name, but she didn't want credit for them—or at least she didn't want the credit to go to her. She wanted every stroke of kindness to be traced back to the one who inspired it in the first place: Cheyenne.

Over time, Joanne realized that other people—not just parents but anyone who has experienced a death—might want to continue to honor the name of their departed loved one through kindness. She created cards that can be personalized and given to a person who is wondering where an unexpected kindness came from. They read, "This Random Act of Kindness Done in Loving Memory of _____." To date, one million cards have been distributed. (To learn more, visit www. missfoundation.org.)

Naming and Healing

My friend Tawnya, whose son Samuel died when he was a day old, tells me that the question, "How many children do you have?" has been so painful and confusing for her that for years she avoided old friends who did not know about Samuel's death. She could not bear to have them ask, as she didn't want to lie, yet telling the truth was often awkward and led to unintended consequences.

Sometimes when people asked her how many children she had she would answer truthfully, that she had two, Natalia, age three, and Samuel, who died after just one day. People did not know how to respond to this information, and sometimes she found herself in the odd position of having to comfort them.

Five years after Samuel's death, Tawnya no longer avoids old friends. She doesn't need to only be around those who know—she can branch out and renew old contacts. She feels that the ability to speak Samuel's name publicly is a sign that she is slowly moving toward healing, moving forward even if the path will never be smooth or straight.

As I explored those Japanese rituals for children who have died, I wondered if there might be a Christian parallel—a tangible place for grief and remembrance for the unborn or stillborn. A simple Google search reveals that there are statues and cemeteries for the unborn. But I was particularly intrigued by the work of two Orthodox monks in California who have created a garden for the unborn.

The monks sent me photos of their garden and the community that built it—showing small children with shovels, older men and women pouring cement for a flagstone staircase that curves up the hillside toward the garden. The staircase is flanked by occasional icons— two-dimensional images of saints—as if to suggest that the unborn do not wait alone. There is a prayer cell dug out of the gigantic stump of a fallen redwood, and there are chairs for weary parents to sit in. Everything about this garden is oriented toward quiet, peaceful reflection.

Just behind their chapel, and beneath a grove of gigantic redwoods, is a resting place for the tiniest of caskets—those of the unborn. In cases of early miscarriage or abortion there is often no body to bury. For these littlest ones, there is simply a stone with the baby's name. This serene and shady area invites parents to connect with the reality of all that has happened and all that they hope toward.

These tiny bodies, tucked into the same fertile soil that nurtured the ancient redwoods, are like seeds. They appear dead, but I trust that one day they will wake. This belief illumines my passion for naming— seeing the seed, believing that life, in the end, will crack it open.

Naming the child is an act that we do once, and then again and again and again, as we speak the child into reality. The name unlocks the memory, and also holds it close, reminding the world of our own unique and precious child: a baby that could only be born once, that the world will never stop aching for until all things are restored.

Suggestions for Naming the Child:

• If you are pregnant and receive the news that your baby will die, name the baby. The name will allow you to bond, to speak to your baby, and to speak about your baby in a way that will make his or her presence real to others.

- Many parents who experienced the death of their child at birth or shortly afterward wish that they had a special item that their baby had used as a memento. Consider having older siblings decorate a bib or piece of clothing with the baby's name for the baby to wear and then for the family to keep. You might also wish to adorn a quilt with your baby's name and the meanings behind it. This quilt could be used to wrap the baby after birth and then retained as a keepsake for future generations.

- Sometimes it can be difficult to name a baby, especially if it died through miscarriage and you do not know the sex. If you are open to prayer, consider praying for a name and asking others to pray for one with you.

- After the baby has died, there are many ways to keep that baby's name alive. Include that baby's name in holiday cards, letters to family and friends, perhaps even on a piece of jewelry.

- Purchase kindness cards from the M.I.S.S. Foundation: www.missfoundation.org. These cards can help you to create a legacy of love and generosity in the name of your child.

Pregnancy and Birth

You will give birth to her soon, and it may be like getting your period, or it may be like any other labor, with water breaking, with contractions and release, and it will be a sad, sad birth. But angels are present when babies are born—when all babies are born. Take comfort in their presence. Listen for the rush of wings.

—Claudia Mair Burney

When I was nine months pregnant with my firstborn, Anna, I woke up early and walked down the hill to the seminary chapel for Matins. It was a crisp morning at the cusp of fall. After the service I waddled back up the hill, stopping to catch my breath under a denim sky. The sky itself seemed to groan, and my friend and I looked up, "Doesn't that plane seem awfully low?" he asked.

We were in Westchester County, New York, glimpsing the first plane that was to smash into the World Trade Center on September 11, 2001. For years afterward, it was that steak of gray groaning in the denim sky that came back to me in my dreams. That, and the knowledge that it was time to stop pretending we were safe.

A few weeks later, I remember walking through the quiet streets of our neighborhood with the newborn Anna nestled in a sling. I remember looking at the stately homes, flags flapping in the wind, wondering if everyone had made it home safely that day. A gray-haired man carried his trash out to the curb and saw me approaching with the sling. He peered at Anna, touched the top of her head and asked how old she was. "Seven days," I said. "God bless you," he said, shaking his head sadly.

That walk comes back to me vividly, because of the conversation inside of my head, the wonder at Anna, and the terror at the world I had brought her into, a world that had shifted suddenly beneath my feet. I wondered if I had made a terrible mistake, if Anna would have to suffer for my naiveté.

But, of course, September 11, 2001, was one possibility I couldn't have planned for during my pregnancy. And looking back, I know that the world in which Anna was conceived was not the same one into which she was born. It was two worlds, and always will be—the one before and the one after.

September 11 was an unprecedented disaster on American soil, but on a micro level, a similar split occurs in the pregnancies of hundreds of thousands of women around the world—a before and an after—the innocence they had before all the cards were laid out on the table, the sweet silent hopefulness of the early weeks before the bleeding started or the cramping began or before the diagnosis was made, before the knowledge set in that this baby they'd been given to carry might not be theirs to keep.

I mentioned my friend Rachelle Mee-Chapman in the last chapter, and the horrible moment in her fifth month of pregnancy when an ultrasound revealed all that was wrong with her son. The doctor offered to book the "procedure" for that afternoon. "Do you mean an abortion?" Rachelle asked.

This idea troubled her because she knew that Simeon was developed enough to feel pain. She had received so much bleak information, she couldn't see any other way through. She quickly agreed, but her husband intervened, saying they needed time to make a decision.

They chose to gather more information through genetic testing and another ultrasound. This time, a Catholic doctor was on call, and she suggested that they induce labor instead. That way, Rachelle and Paul could hold their baby. Still Rachelle was worried that even labor would be painful for Simeon because his chest was open and he lacked an abdominal wall.

When a bed finally opened in the maternity ward, Rachelle was relieved to find out that the same Catholic doctor was on call. She suggested another ultrasound, which provided a little more relief. On the screen before them, they saw that his tiny heart had stopped beating—Simeon had left on his own.

Rachelle describes his birth this way:

> *He was very tiny, about the length of my arm from my elbow to my wrist. The nurse, nervous and new to this kind of sorrow, had eventually managed to wrap him in blankets, one small arm extending outside of the heap, his hand so frail I was afraid to touch it lest I tear his fragile skin. We had wept so many times for him, our doomed son. Tears in the dark sonogram*

room; tears when my knees collapsed in the hospital stairway; tears when we told our parents; tears as we waited all the long week to see him delivered; tears in the cold procedures room as the new nurse fled and we were left to deliver our baby alone.

There were more tears now, as we played him special songs, anointed his head in our own private baptism, sang him chants from my Lutheran childhood. Tears as we set him in the infant warmer—now disconnected and cold—to say goodbye. . . . On this day I remember Simeon David Chapman, who made me a mother, who is this mother's only son.

Rachelle's experience is common. In many cases, when diagnostic tests reveal that the baby has serious chromosomal problems, the pregnancy seems like a dead end, with only one option. But the doctor on call helped Rachelle and Paul to see another possibility— that labor could be induced instead. While it would still be a heart-wrenching experience, they would be able to hold their son after he was born.

In *Expecting Adam*, Martha Beck struggles over the implications of genetic testing during pregnancy. While she remains committed to a women's right to choose throughout the book, her growing bond with her son makes her unwilling to consider termination when he is diagnosed with Down syndrome.

The story unfolds against the backdrop of Harvard, where both she and her husband are graduate students, where the very notion of bringing a baby with Down syndrome into the world is considered abhorrent by many of their peers and professors. Early in the book, when her husband says that terminating babies with birth defects is a way to ease the suffering of everyone involved—she realizes that her thinking on the subject is beginning to shift.

"Look, John, it's not as though we're deciding whether or not to have a baby. We're deciding what *kind* of baby we're willing to accept," she says. "If it's perfect in every way, keep it. If it is doesn't fit the right specifications, whoosh! Out it goes."

She tells her husband that she worries about where the line will be drawn as technology advances and more and more information becomes available about the unborn. What will constitute a permissible reason to terminate? What about a fetus with a genetic predisposition toward alcoholism, homosexuality, or manic depression?

Technology is advancing faster than our ability to meaningfully reflect on all of the implications of our choices. Sometimes it can be difficult to see clearly all that is and all that could be. Part of the beauty of *Expecting Adam* is Beck's suggestion that life is not exactly as it seems—it is actually *more* than it seems.

Before Martha Beck published her book as autobiography, she first wrote it as a novel with this synopsis: "This is the story of two driven Harvard academics who found out mid-pregnancy that their unborn son would be retarded. . . . They decided to allow their baby to be born. What they did not realize is that they themselves were the ones who would be 'born,' infants in a new world where magic is commonplace, Harvard professors are the slow learners and retarded babies are the master teachers."

Heartbreak and Hope

Every parent I have spoken with has experienced some kind of "birth" through the process of struggling to bring a child into the world, even when the child died within the first few months of pregnancy. The transformation is not just emotional or spiritual, but also physical. The very act of bearing a child changes a woman's body in all sorts of ways, both known and unknown. It is believed that each baby a woman bears—even those that don't come to term—will leave behind remnant stem cells that will increase the mother's resistance to certain autoimmune disorders. In a very real way, that baby never totally leaves.

Lyn's first child, Rebecca, died of trisomy 18. At Lyn's twenty-week ultrasound, the technician felt there was reason for concern and requested that her doctor review the images immediately. Her doctor agreed to see her right away. Sobbing, Lyn walked through the waiting room of the obstetrician's office. There she saw a sea of faces, women in the full glow of their pregnancies, watching her. They were innocent in a way that Lyn would never be again.

The only way a sure diagnosis of Lyn's baby could be made would be through amniocentesis. Her doctor outlined the procedure and risks: a needle would be inserted into the womb so that fluids could be taken. There would be a slight chance of miscarriage. They chose to have this procedure done. When the needle was carefully inserted into her womb to take the fluids, her baby flinched at the intrusion.

The amniocentesis yielded the results that Lyn and Rob feared. Their baby was deemed "incompatible with life." Lyn and Rob were told that if their baby was born alive—and that was a big if—she would have only a four percent chance of making it to her first birthday.

The physician asked, in light of the bleak prognosis, if they wanted to terminate. Lyn and Rob could barely speak when asked this question. That day, their in-laws drove into town to grieve with them and to help them work through their decision. Lyn's father-in-law said the words Lyn had not had the courage to voice. He said, "You know, perhaps you should consider it."

But Lyn's husband, Rob, shook his head. He said, "This baby belongs to God and we must trust him to help us through."

Rob's words marked a turning point for the couple. They named the baby Rebecca Faith, and they began to speak to her and call her by name—and by nicknames. "She was Becca, Rebecca, and Rebecca Faith," Lyn says.

One of the most surprising aspects of the pregnancy for Lyn was that although she had been told their unborn baby was "severely retarded," Rebecca moved at the sound of her name and responded with kicks and rolls to their nudges and voices.

When Lyn didn't feel Becca moving, she would ask, then beg her, to show that she was okay. But on two different occasions, Becca would not move. No amount of sugary orange soda (drunk by Lyn) or prodding from her mother would make her move.

Both times, Lyn called her husband at work and asked him to come home. She lay down on her bed and Rob put his face near her belly and said, "Becca, you're scaring mommy. Could you move a little so that she knows you're okay?" And both times Becca kicked immediately as if to say, "I'm okay, I'm right here."

At forty-one weeks, Lyn and Rob went to the doctor's office for a routine appointment. Lyn hadn't felt Becca moving that day, but she wasn't especially worried— not until her doctor couldn't find a heartbeat. At that point, he ordered an ultrasound, which confirmed the couples' fears: Becca had died. The doctor told her that she would deliver in the morning. He told her to go home and rest. "You're going to need a good night's sleep," he said.

Lyn and Rob went home to a houseful of people who were there to grieve and pray with them. At 10:45 p.m., their pastor arrived, startling everyone. "I hope it's okay that I came," he said. "I just heard the news."

That night, in the wee hours, the contractions began. Lyn and Rob headed out to the hospital, and she gave birth several hours later. As Becca came into the world—still and beautiful—peace filled the room. The nurses encouraged Lyn and Rob to hold Rebecca for as long as they wanted. So Rob and Lyn snuggled with her as family members and people from the church filed into the room. "My pastor said he'd never seen a room so full of sadness and peace," Lyn says. There were laughter and tears, a community of love surrounding Becca and her parents.

As Lyn later reflected on that strange quietness and peace, she said, "That was a gift from God, that came through prayer and trusting him through the entire process." After many hours with their Becca, Rob and Lyn let her go, knowing the longer they held her, the harder it would be to release her. They found a funeral home that was willing to cremate her at no charge—the funeral director had experienced the death of one of his own children and was unwilling to charge in such circumstances.

Five days passed. The couple made it through Becca's memorial service, and then, to Lyn's surprise and horror, she discovered that her milk was coming in. But she and Rob needed some kind of distraction, so she wrapped herself in an ace bandage and put on a heavy sweater to go to the movies.

They stared at the screen together, numb with shock. As they left the theatre, Lyn realized that her milk had seeped through the ace bandage and through her heavy wool sweater. Her aching breasts were as hard as rocks and she was wet and clammy. "It was insult on top of injury," she says.

Shortly after Rebecca's death, Lyn and Rob began to try for another child. Month after month, Lyn grieved the baby that she would not hold in her arms. During this time, a close friend and her sister-in-law both gave birth to healthy babies, and Lyn wanted to love them and not feel resentful. "But those emotions were just part of my reality," she says.

Finally, on New Year's Day, Lyn and Rob talked about their dreams for the coming year. They were not in the same place emotionally: Rob remained stubbornly hopeful, believing that God still had something good in store for them. Although Lyn was also hopeful, she was still grieving and it was hard for her to see the bigger picture.

Rob took her hand and said, "Let's pray that within the year we will be holding our second child in our arms." Lyn was willing, but she could barely restrain herself from rolling her eyes at his optimism. For her to give birth within the year would mean that she would have to conceive within two months.

But by February, Lyn wasn't feeling quite right. Her cycles still seemed irregular, and her body felt kind of *off*. She contacted the receptionist at her physician's office, the same person who had checked her in for that devastating ultrasound more than a year before. She told the receptionist she wanted to make an appointment because of her worrisome irregularity. The receptionist said, "Well, I'm just going to hope you're pregnant."

Within ten minutes, a close friend called to report that she had just found out that she was pregnant. "And

I hope you're pregnant too—and you know what? I think you are."

Lyn took a pregnancy test, and she saw two pink lines. She headed to the doctor's office for confirmation. She was pregnant! Her doctor asked her to make a follow-up appointment. That caring receptionist checked the calendar and said, "How would April 13 be for you?" Lyn agreed to that date, but as she was walking across the office she realized that April 13 would have been Becca's first birthday.

The day that Rebecca would have turned one was bittersweet. That morning, she heard the heartbeat of her second child—strong and steady—the promise of new life to come. And that night, as the sun set over the Pacific, Lyn and Rob took what remained of Becca—a film canister containing a tablespoon of ashes—out to a pier. It was a windy night, but as they prayed, the wind grew calm and a gentle breeze finally carried Becca out to sea.

Devastation Trail

I live in Hawaii, not far from the world's only drive-up active volcano. One of the most fascinating hikes in Volcanoes National Park curves through Devastation Trail, which takes you over sun-baked lava pierced by skeletal trees. The hard lava crunches beneath your feet like ice-crusted snow as you walk over the remains of a verdant forest.

But even on Devastation Trail, life is making a comeback. Tiny shoots of green and brown are coming up from the lava, slowly, steadily kneading it into rich, fertile soil, pregnant with possibility.

I mentioned our friends Tawnya and Nick in the last chapter, whose baby Samuel died when he was one day old. After his death, Nick and Tawnya discovered that there was a strong chance that one of them could be a carrier of the genetic issue that caused Samuel's abnormality. They chose not to have the tests that would give them this exact percentage of risk, but they were told it could be as much as 50 percent.

As they struggled over the possibility of conceiving another baby only to have it die, one genetic counselor offered them these helpful words, "No matter what, no matter who you are, you always have a greater chance of having a healthy baby."

As they navigated these unknown and fearful questions, my husband and Nick went out for a meal. As Nick shared his fears, my husband said, "Nick, don't be afraid to try for another. Even though life is sometimes wounded, sometimes shorter than we'd like it to be—it is still bigger than death."

Just this past week, Nick and Tawnya proved those words true, yet again, as they gave birth to their second healthy baby girl, Amelia Jane.

Still, while many parents who experience the death of an infant will go on to bear more biologically, not every couple that longs for children will give birth to them. Some will chose to adopt, and still others will become informal parents to all those in need of care. There are as many ways to mother as there are to love.

Mother Maria Skobtsova, a recently canonized Orthodox saint, discovered her vocation after her daughter died of meningitis. She became "aware of a new and special, broad and all-embracing motherhood," as one expert has put it. She went on to say that she saw a "new road before me and a new meaning in life, to be a mother for all, for all who need maternal care, assistance or protection."

Mother Skobtsova's maternal desire led her into the streets of Paris, where she sought out anyone in need of love—the homeless, those struggling with alcoholism, as well as the orphaned children of Holocaust victims. Her love ultimately landed her into a concentration camp, where she died alongside those she had chosen to cherish as her own flesh and blood.

Mothering is an expansive vocation. It grows as we do, and it is not limited by biology or genetics. It can make mothers of all of us, even if we don't know what form this will take. But the path can be rough and windy. It can be so much harder to get there than we imagined.

For those who are still on Devastation Trail, I offer these words, written by my friend Claudia Mair Burney, who, after experiencing two miscarriages and one stillbirth, wrote these words to a pregnant friend with a bleak prognosis:

You can ask why, but don't be surprised if you never get an answer. Sometimes you don't. Sometimes it's just life on the wrong side of heaven, Sweetie. It's tainted over here, and it can get really dark and cold sometimes. And don't go looking for a lesson in all of this. God doesn't need to take away your baby to teach you.

Some days the peace that God gives will be your sanity, but there may be days, well after you think the worst is over, that you may be like your evil twin here, the bassinet assassin. Those days are okay, too. Whatever you feel is simply what you feel. Don't judge yourself or any emotion, and remember that the face of grief can change, day-by-day, moment-by-moment.

You may never get over it. I assure you, you will feel like you again, and there will come a time when that raw and bleeding wound will become a dull ache that you don't even notice most days. But it never leaves completely. And if it does, tell me how, because it's been nine years and I still feel it. I'd rather they were here with me, even on my worst days.

You said to me, when you called tonight, after hearing me weeping on your answering machine, "She can't come back to me, but I will go to her." And you will go to her, and she'll be running and you'll be running to her. But how we'll miss her in this world. And we will remember her name. I stop and say it even as I write this. God bless and keep you loved until we get Home, baby girl. We will always remember your name.

Suggestions for Pregnancy
When the Baby Might Not Survive:

- Take profile photos during the pregnancy and keep a journal. These memories will give you a little glimpse into your baby's unique personality and your own experience of him or her.

- Prepare a CD of comforting songs to play during the labor and afterward, as you grieve. Consider playing those songs during your pregnancy for your baby so that they will connect you to memories of him or her.

- Save everything—ultrasound images, the positive pregnancy test, lists of baby names, and letters from family and friends.

- Advocate for yourself during the pregnancy and birth. Although doctors may recommend pregnancy termination, it may be preferable to induce labor, both for the mother's body and for the sake of the baby. Seek a doctor who is sensitive to your concerns and convictions.

- Contact NILMDTS (www.nowilaymedownto sleep.org) to inquire about the possibility of having a volunteer photographer take photos of you and your family members holding the baby. This service is available in many cities for babies born at twenty-five weeks, or at the discretion of medical personnel.

- If you ask a friend or family member take photos, use black and white or sepia tone, as color photos under fluorescent lights rarely do a newborn justice.

 *Touch*

I looked at your perfect, lifeless body. You were so beautiful. Your skin was flawless and you had curly, ebony hair. You were my largest newborn, weighing 8 pounds, and certainly the healthiest appearing of all my children. You had a double chin and rolls of fat around your wrists. That made it so difficult to understand what had happened. You looked like you were asleep. . . . With a mother's love, I knew I had to make my first and last memories with you now.

—Joanne Cacciatore

When Daria and Father Stephen's first child, Kathryn, died just before labor, their friend Vera came into their hospital room and said, "Hold her. If you do you will be eternally grateful. I didn't and I will always wish I had."

"Vera gave us a gift, and we, in turn, offered that to our families because it wasn't just us who were hurting," Father Stephen says. The death of an infant isn't just experienced by the parents, although their grief is certainly the most acute. It also sends ripples through families and communities.

Some of Father Stephen and Daria's family members didn't want to go to the morgue, but his parents did, and they just held Kathryn. Her skin was mottled and she was wrapped in a waterproof blanket because the processes of death had already begun to set in. "Still, my dad couldn't stop touching her. It took a lot of coaxing to get him to let her go."

Experts say that touch is both the earliest sense to develop in an embryo and the last sense to go when a person is dying. Long after we can't speak or see, we can feel the warmth of a human hand on our arm.

In my Eastern Orthodox tradition, we say goodbye with our hands. When I was new to the church, I was not at all comfortable with this custom. The first Orthodox funeral I attended was for a two-year-old boy who died from a heart defect. The casket was open, and every member of the church went forward and kissed his forehead or touched his chest. So much love was poured out onto him this way, and yet I had never touched a dead body before, and the idea of it was unnerving.

But after more than a decade in the church, I've grown to love this farewell ritual. A few years ago, a close friend died in a car accident. I will never forget how the priests who served at his funeral came forward one by one at the end of the service, bending to kiss his forehead. This tender gesture spoke to me in a way that nothing else could.

Over time, I've begun to think that we say goodbye with our hands because it helps us. The dead don't need our kisses, although I doubt they mind. Still, our finite minds cannot grasp why or how a two-year-old child could die. So when our minds fail, our bodies take over, groping in the darkness for a way through this tearful valley, reaching for that person we loved and caressing them even as we let them go.

Because I've grown more and more committed to the idea of the tactile goodbye, I was surprised to discover that there is currently a debate over whether parents who have experienced the death of a baby should be "allowed" to hold their deceased infant. Some physicians point to studies that suggest that holding a deceased baby increases the chances of maternal anxiety and depression during subsequent pregnancies.

Dr. Joanne Cacciatore is the mother of Cheyenne, who died twenty minutes before birth. She is also the founder of the M.I.S.S. (Mothers in Support and Solidarity) Foundation, a professor at the University of Arizona, and an expert in traumatic loss and child death in families. And she is floored that such a debate even exists. She cannot imagine how anyone other than the parent has the right to determine if mothers and fathers should be allowed to hold their own children. "Imagine if the child were ten years old—would anyone dare to tell the parent that they could not hold her?" she says.

Her research and experience has convinced her that it can be very helpful for parents to engage in "farewell rituals" that mirror the instinctive ritual parents engage in upon the birth of a live baby. The parents can stroke the baby's hair and cheeks, count the fingers and toes, smell the top of the head and examine and memorize every part of him or her. All of these tactile experiences help imprint the infant on the mother, help her to realize that this baby is separate from herself, a revelation that will be helpful during the grieving process.

According to Dr. Cacciatore, hospitals and medical professionals have an ethical obligation to facilitate farewell rituals, while never pressuring parents who do not feel comfortable holding their babies. Seeing and touching the baby makes it real to the parent. "How can you grieve the death of an infant if it does not yet feel real to you?" she asks.

Dr. Cacciatore has sat with hundreds of families of every race and creed and culture shortly after the death of their infants. She's been with mothers and fathers and sisters and grandparents who were Hindu, Buddhist, Atheist, Christian, Sikh, Zorastrian, Jewish, Native American, Latino, and African American. Through these experiences with the bereaved, she has seen firsthand that many mothers are afraid to hold their own babies, even if on some level, they desire it. She has learned to recognize that fear and to help women overcome it. Her approach is simple. She'll sit with the mother for a time in her hospital room. Then she'll say, "You don't have to hold your baby. It's okay if you don't want to. But could I?" In every case, the mother has agreed.

Dr. Cacciatore will hold the baby in her arms, stroke the baby's cheek, and look lovingly at him or her as she speaks with the mother. While she does this, the mother will often interrupt and say, "Could I hold her?" And then she'll pass the baby back to the mother, who will begin to caress and study her baby.

While this concrete, tangible act of holding the baby may sometimes cause anxiety during subsequent pregnancies, it is an experience that parents remember with gratitude. "So many times over the years, Daria and I have fallen back on the knowledge that we held Kathryn," Father Stephen says. "We touched her, we held her close, and then we offered that experience to our family as well."

By holding their baby, the parents claim him or her as their own. In the chaos and confusion after death, against the stark backdrop of a hospital room with its beeping machines and fluorescent lights, the parents can say with their bodies—this precious baby is mine. They can let their instincts guide them to whatever feels most natural; they can smell the baby's soft forehead or stroke his or her downy forearms. They can feel the weight of the child they knew in the womb as he or she rests in their arms one last time.

In so doing, parents, quite unknowingly, reverse a troubling trend. As Joanne Cacciatore pointed out, "Over the last century, our society has taken the two most important experiences of life—birth and death— out of the loving hands of family and placed them under the impersonal care of institutions."

I know of a church in Alaska where death is handled completely in-house. The priest, family, and friends come together to pray the dying person over the threshold, and after the death occurs, a group of women assemble to wash the body, a man from the community builds a simple pine casket, and everyone comes together once more to lower the casket into the ground, and to shovel the soil.

This physical, emotional, and spiritual work helps the community begin to reconcile themselves to the reality of what has happened. By refusing to outsource the concrete details of caring for the dead, they can see and feel the truth—that death is real and irreversible and that the life they grieve together is unrepeatable and sacred. They have accompanied someone they loved through that critical threshold, and when that time comes for them, they will not face it alone. They know that love transcends the grave because they have lived it. But what I can't help but wonder is—who is helped most by these rituals—the dead or the living?

Struggling to Hold On

While it may be most ideal to hold the baby—either after the baby has died or while the baby is in his or her final hours, it can be an agonizing experience. My friends Tawnya and Nick held their son Samuel as he was dying. The emotional pain, coupled with Tawnya's exhaustion from the traumatic birth, made it difficult. During that day, which was both excruciatingly long and short, Tawnya struggled against an almost irresistible urge to fall asleep, to escape the pain of witnessing Samuel's suffering.

And yet, she did what was most natural to her. She unwrapped his tightly swaddled blanket, unbuttoned her shirt, and let him snuggle against her chest during his last day of life. He leaned against her like that for many hours, basking in the warmth of skin-on-skin contact.

She describes the experience this way: "His sweet baby body. It makes life more real to me. Loving touch confirms the sacredness of life. But it was painful and hard to hold him, waiting for life to end: hearing the labor of his breathing, knowing it could—and would—stop at any moment."

Tawnya says that she understands why doctors sometimes want to "protect" parents from this agony. Now that she has two daughters, she understands the vast difference between holding a dying infant and holding one who is awakening to life in this world. "I could see why you would want to protect someone from that—it was hard to hold him. To look on the suffering of your sweet innocent baby, to know that he was hurting, to know that he could barely take his next breath—who wants to see that? And yet to miss it would have been to deprive myself, not of some great memory, but of the ability to do the one small thing I could do for my son in this life."

When Touch Is Not Possible

The ache is also great when parents do not have the opportunity to hold their babies. Sometimes a miscarriage occurs long before the baby's form can be clearly made out. Sometimes there is only tissue to bury. Other times a baby is born so critically ill that the child is whisked away before the parents have had a chance to hold him. And sometimes, hospital staff are not aware of—or sensitive to—the parents' desire to say goodbye with their hands.

I was with another friend just after her three-month-old baby died, and I remember the agonizing swishing sound as she pumped her breast milk and let it drip down the drain. We ache in so many ways after we lose a child, but one of the greatest aches is the physical one—our bodies, which nurtured and held these babies as they grew inside, expects contact. A mother's body, which has been gearing up for the work of mothering for a lifetime, will often be profoundly disoriented and frustrated when a baby dies.

The best we can do for the dying—and for those who have died—is to linger with them a bit, to touch them if we can. When touch is not possible, for whatever reason, we can try to fill in the gaps with our loving thoughts and prayerful intentions.

In Henri Nouwen's book *Our Greatest Gift: A Meditation on Dying and Caring*, he compares the process of dying to the work of being a trapeze artist, with God as the catcher. He asked a trapeze artist named Rodleigh about his work as a flyer. Rodleigh said, "The secret is that the flyer does nothing and the catcher does everything. The worst thing a flyer can do is to try to catch the catcher. . . . A flyer must fly and a catcher must catch, and the flyer must trust, with outstretched arms, that his catcher will be there for him."

When we care for our infants as they leave this world, we offer them courage to make their final leap. According to Nouwen, our love for the dying conveys this essential and liberating message: "Don't be afraid. Remember that you are the beloved child of God. He will be there when you make your long jump. Don't try to grab him, he will grab you. Just stretch out your arms and hands and trust, trust, trust."

Suggestions for the Moments after Your Baby Has Died:

- If your baby is born with his or her eyes closed, do not be afraid to open them if you wish. This will be your only chance to look into them.

- Although it will be painful, include older siblings and family members in the experience, if possible. Most parents report that children are surprisingly adept at coping with death, especially if they are not excluded from the critical moments.

- Consider bathing and dressing your baby and wrapping him or her in a blanket that you can take home from the hospital. You may wish to remove the hospital ID tag as a memento, or clip a lock of hair. Many parents have been comforted by the smell of their babies, which lingers for a time on blankets and clothing.

- If your physician is reluctant to facilitate a farewell ritual, just calmly assert your wishes, knowing that you retain the right to hold your own child. You may need to arrange in advance to have friends or family members advocate for you.

- You may want to invite extended family, such as parents, grandparents, or godparents to hold the baby as well. By allowing them to share in these painful and sacred moments, you will help them to better understand what has occurred.

 *Words*

*With an anxious and hurried look, he searches among
the crowds to find if there is just one person who
will listen to him. But the crowds hurry by without
noticing him or his trouble. Yet it is such an immense,
illimitable grief. Should his heart break and the grief
pour out, it would flow over the whole earth, and yet
no one sees it.*

—ANTON CHEKHOV

*T*wo years ago a friend died in a car accident
and his wife, Rachel, asked me to come and
be with her as she faced her first night alone in the
apartment they had shared. That night comes back to
me in vivid detail: Nate's flannel shirt hanging casually
over a chair as if at any moment he would walk back
through to door and claim it, the eerie feeling of absence
and presence in that apartment, and the wind, which
howled all night long over the central Illinois prairie,
tearing the last autumn leaves from the trees.

We barely slept that night, as Rachel drifted in and out
of sleep, moaning and crying intermittently. At times I
was frightened, because the veil that separates the living
and the dead seemed to have lifted. I felt exposed and
vulnerable, powerless in the face of something much
bigger than myself, perched at the edge of all that I
knew.

As that sleepless night wore on, I became more and
more exhausted, nearly delirious at times. I kept trying

to focus on Rachel, to be present with her, despite the increasingly strong waves of sleep threatening to pull me under.

At some point I realized that my only context for understanding what was happening was my own experience of laboring ten hours to bring my older daughter Anna into the world. I didn't have the courage to bring up this thought with Rachel, but I did want to know if anyone else had experienced the same feeling. When I got home I did a Google search and found out that, sure enough, there are both "death doulas" and "death midwifes" who support dying people and their caregivers as they cross over the threshold. Not surprisingly, most of the people who do this work are women trained as labor midwives who transition into care for the dying and the bereaved as they age and begin to see the need.

A few months after that long night, I gathered my courage and called Rachel. I told her that if I hadn't known better, I would have thought she was in labor. She didn't miss a beat. "That's right," she said. "I was laboring to bring Nate into the next world."

If you've ever experienced childbirth, you know that laboring women can become downright fierce as the contractions take hold. They may or may not appreciate levity. They might withdraw into themselves, seeking some hidden reserves of strength as they try to bear the pain and bring new life into the world. They reserve the right to punch, kick, swear, or do anything else that might seem inappropriate under normal circumstances. The physical, emotional, and spiritual work involved in the labor process requires complete and total concentration.

Ever since that night with Rachel, I understand that the bereaved are not unlike women in labor. They are experiencing excruciating pain. They are in the grips of a process that they cannot control, pulled over rocks by a current that they cannot stop. They do not know when (or if) the pain will end. Perhaps they don't know if there is anything on the other side of the agony—and the agony at this point is total, and all consuming. Just like a laboring woman, their perceptions are focused and heightened, and sensations are acute. They might feel like they are dying at one moment, more painfully alive than ever before in the next. They know that there is no escape—the only way out is through.

If you think of bereaved parents as if they are experiencing protracted labor, you can understand why words have such a profound effect, why careless ones can provoke rage or tears, why pat clichés are so unwelcome. But just as many women in labor need a companion to help them through, so too, the bereaved can be helped by the presence of a loving friend. But they need that friend to put his or her own agenda aside and to be present with them in their pain.

My friend Juliana, who experienced a miscarriage at twelve and a half weeks, described an irritating encounter shortly after the miscarriage. A friend came to visit under the appearance of coming to offer condolences, but the whole time she was there, she chattered about frivolous things. "I wanted to say, 'My son just died. Could you shut up about that stupid video game?'" Juliana says.

Many people imagine that they can help the bereaved by attempting to distract them. Try this with a laboring woman, and you might be injured! Most bereaved parents don't want to be distracted, either. They want to be with their grief because the labor of grief takes everything they have and connects them to their child. They have no choice but to see the process through, and at times they will need companions to walk beside them.

The Wisdom of Silence

In the Jewish tradition, after a death close family and friends will come and sit silently with the bereaved person. They are doing what is called "sitting shiva," observing a weeklong period of mourning. Sometimes they will even sit on low chairs or on the floor as a symbolic way of being very "low" with the weight of the grief. During that most intense period of grief immediately following the death, the bereaved are not expected to bathe or read Torah or have intercourse. Normal life stops while they let the reality of what has happened sink in. Traditionally, visitors are not supposed to speak, as words always fall short in the face of the experience of loss. These are good practices, and helpful to the bereaved. The work of being a silent witness to these sacred moments of life is an art—one that seems to have been largely lost in the rush of modern society.

It is awful to witness the pain of another person and not be able to do anything about it. But this is just what the bereaved need—a person to walk beside them and hear them without trying to fix it. What has happened is unfixable in the temporal sense.

From a Judeo-Christian perspective, death is no friend. It was not part of the original plan back in Eden. It is a distortion and a perversion, rooted in the fall. A Jewish friend tells me that at her brother's funeral the rabbi said that within the Jewish tradition there are no prescribed prayers for the death of a child because this kind of death is not supposed to happen.

For this reason, platitudes, easy phrases such as, "It was God's will," or, "Be comforted by your memories," or, "Time will heal your wounds," don't help. Some of these things may be partly true, but the bereaved need space to have their own epiphanies. They do not welcome the easy assurances of the uninitiated.

In "The Eldest Child," Maeve Brennan describes a mother after the death of her three-day-old baby. The mother, Mrs. Bagot, struggles not just with the loss, but also with her friends and family, who do not want to hear what she has to say. Brennan writes:

When she spoke for any length of time they always
silenced her by telling her it was God's will. She had
accepted God's will all her life without argument, and
she was not arguing now, but she knew that what had
happened was not finished and she was sure that it was
not God's will that she be left in this bewilderment.
. . . All she wanted to do was say how she felt, but they
mentioned God's will as if they were slamming a door
between her and some territory that was forbidden to
her.

Grieving parents need an opportunity to be with their
grief and to be heard in it. Friends do well if they come
to the home of a grieving parent with flowers and food
but no agenda, no pat clichés to offer, and especially no
fear. In so many cases, it is fear that keeps us from being
able to hear our friends out when they are describing
their journey through the "forbidden" territory of
anguish.

People are often afraid to face their own fear of death,
and being with the bereaved forces an encounter with
the inevitable. Even those who genuinely want to help
might be tempted to push the grievers toward hope
before they're ready.

But perhaps the most helpful response is to allow the
process to unfold as it will, to be a witness to the pain
and rage without attempting to "fix it." As Catholic
priest and author Richard John Neuhaus once wrote,
"There is a time simply to be present to death—whether

one's own or that of others—without any felt urgencies about doing something about it or getting over it." It requires courage to walk with another through the rugged, uncharted cavern of grief and let them grope toward their own answers. But this is ultimately the most hopeful—and helpful—response.

Struggling for Words

Most of the grieving parents I have met not only struggled with words that were said (or not said) to them, but they also had to search for a vocabulary to express all that they were feeling. Many were uneasy with the term loss as a way to describe the death of an infant.

For Rachelle Mee-Chapman the word lost did not express her experience. "I remember coming home from school once after a long day of well-wishers and explanations, and sobbing to my husband Paul, 'Simeon is not LOST. I didn't misplace him. He's just gone.'" Rachelle feels it is more appropriate to say "he died" than he was "lost." She's particularly wary of the spiritual implications of the word, because lost does not convey the reality of a safe afterlife.

Counselors say that the term lost is particularly problematic because it suggests blame—that the mother "lost" her child and if she was somehow more careful the baby would still be here. To say that an infant died is to say that something occurred within that infant's body—nobody is to blame. Nobody "lost" the child. It just happened; the baby died.

In the end, terms like lost or passed away are often our attempts to whitewash a harsh and troubling reality. As C.S. Lewis wrote in *A Grief Observed* after the death of his wife: "It is hard to have patience with people who say, 'There is no death' or 'Death doesn't matter.' There is death. And whatever it is matters. And whatever happens has consequences that are irrevocable and irreversible. You might as well say that birth doesn't matter." Similarly, most of the consolations we might offer after an older person has died are a poor fit for the death of a child. We can't say that the baby had a long and fruitful life, and there are not stores of memories to draw from. Instead, there is just the jagged edge of a life that ended long before we expected it to—that was taken from us in a way we could not have imagined.

Sometimes words bring more pain than they do healing. Often when I ask parents if they remember any comments that were hurtful to them, they are able to vividly relate a conversation that didn't sit well. Father Stephen Loposky remembers something that was said to him as friends and family filed through the receiving line after Kathryn's funeral. "Well, that's life," an acquaintance said to him.

"It hurt, angered, and it frustrated me," Father Stephen says. "In a sense, they were right, death is a part of life, and yet it is the part of life that was never supposed to happen. His words demonstrated a total lack of compassion."

As much as bereaved parents struggle with inappropriate words that may have been said to them, they also understand that nobody really knows what to say. There are no words, so people fake it, saying unhelpful things, such as, "You will have other children one day," or, "There was probably something wrong with the baby."

People have always struggled to find the right words after a death. In one of the most ancient tragedies, the biblical tale of Job, after everything is snatched from him in an instant—his children, his riches, his health—friends step in to offer words of consolation. Each friend is more unhelpful than the last until Job is finally forced to run them off his property, saying, "How long will you torment me, and break me in pieces with words?" And Job made no bones about what his friends could do with their platitudes. "Your maxims," Job said, "are proverbs of ashes."

Proverbs of ashes crumble when you hold them up to the light of reality. These are words spoken without experience or knowledge, words that leave a bitter residue behind. Perhaps what grieving parents need most are not words but silence—a willingness to simply acknowledge and be present to the experience with the bereaved.

Rachelle experienced something similar when her son Simeon died. She was in graduate school at the time, and Simeon's death occurred over the summer when many of her friends were away. But in her close-knit community, everyone was concerned, so she found herself having the same sort of uncomfortable conversations repeatedly.

"I had to explain what happened over and over again, and then be prepared to comfort them in their sorrow over our loss. It was very confusing and draining. I was not at all prepared for that part of the experience," she says.

A Time to Mourn

In the rush of modern society, friends and family quickly lose patience with the bereaved, who might in turn lose patience with themselves. The standard expectation is that after a few months, you should be "getting on with things," or beginning to get back into a normal routine. But psychologists say that grieving a death may take as much as two years, and even when the most intensive period of grief comes to an end, the sadness remains. A friend of mine who gave birth to a stillborn baby girl said, "You *can* move on, but she goes with you."

Grieving does tend to last longer than we might imagine, especially for parents who have experienced the death of an infant. Life moves on for others, but for the parents, the grief remains fresh and raw for years. Healing from grief does not mean that you never feel the pain again, but that you have slowly found ways to integrate the reality into your life.

Especially when the loss is fresh, a bereaved parent might pour much of their energy into grieving. Ignore this work, and the grief does not subside, it merely slips beneath the surface of life, ready to burst forth like red, hot lava at the slightest provocation.

People often don't realize how much the pain of a miscarriage or the death of an infant will change a person. As Richard John Neuhaus writes:

> *The worst thing is not the sorrow or the loss or the heartbreak. Worse is to be encountered by death and not to be changed by the encounter. There are pills we can take to get through the experience, but the danger is that we then do not go through the experience but around it. Traditions of wisdom encourage us to stay with death a while. Among observant Jews, for instance, those closest to the deceased observe shiva for seven days following the death. During shiva one does not work, bathe, put on shoes, engage in intercourse, read Torah, or have his hair cut. The first response is to give inconsolable grief its due.*

Grief does shape us, in ways we cannot anticipate or articulate. For a time, we might feel crippled by it, unable to function or to be present to new experiences. It may demand our total attention. C.S. Lewis understood this well. In *A Grief Observed* he compares himself to an amputee. Although the stump of the amputated limb heals over time and the ache begins to lessen, the amputee will never again be able to live as he once did. He will have to find his way toward a new kind of normal. "He will never 'get over it,'" writes Lewis. "He will always be a one-legged man. In every waking moment he will know his handicap. His whole way of life will be changed."

Bereaved parents are not unlike the amputee. They will always remember that they once had a child, that their baby was an inextricable, necessary part of their lives. The death of their child requires a new way of living. They must learn to live again despite this loss in their lives. Like the amputee, they will limp and ache and struggle even as their wound begins to heal.

Words fall short, but death must be given its due. When all we have to offer are "maxims of ashes" we do well to take our cues from the Jewish custom that for the first three days after death, visitors don't speak. They just sit quietly beside their friend as the death sinks in. Upon parting, visitors bow their heads and say, quite simply, "May you find peace among the mourners of Zion."

Suggestions about Words
for Bereaved Parents:

- If someone says something insensitive, it is okay to gently tell them why their comment hurt you or seems untrue.
- Some friends won't have the resources to help you through your grief. Don't be shy about protecting yourself. It is okay to let the answering machine pick up and to ignore e-mails and invitations.

- Keep a journal. You will need a safe place to express your feelings and to capture memories before they fade.
- Attend a grief support group. Experts suggest that you attend at least three meetings, as it may take time to become comfortable in this setting. Visit http://www.missfoundation.org/family to locate a local group or to access online support groups.
- Expect that you will process your grief differently even from those who are closest to you. Give yourself and others space to grieve.
- If the grief becomes overwhelming, consider getting the support of a professional counselor.

 *Care*

Yours was the heart I could have cared most for in this world and yours was the heart that I hoped would also so care for me. For caring, I have learned, is a great gift.

My precious darling, how briefly we were close, and how sad I still become; a blessed sadness though it seems this love, this love . . . but how soft it makes my sounds toward others, and that is good.

I should think now of what you would want from me if I could watch you grow . . . it is happiness isn't it. Yes, it is joy in my eyes for you and this world. I will try. I will try.

And thank you, dear, thank you from the deepest parts of me for the wonderful moments, the extraordinary time, yes time, yes time we had.

—"Yours Was the Heart" by DANIEL LADINSKY

I mentioned Dr. Joanne Cacciatore, in the chapter on touch, and how her fourth child, Cheyenne, died during labor. Fifteen minutes before she was to be born, the doctor could not find a heartbeat. Cheyenne was delivered in silence and placed in her father's arms.

Within two hours, Joanne was released from the hospital. During her short stay, she had no contact with a pastor, social worker, or chaplain. She climbed into her car beside her husband and drove home with the ghosted car seat in the back.

She arrived home to a silent nursery and to three young children who could not understand where their baby sister was. Two days later, Joanne's milk came in. Desperate for help, she called local support groups for bereaved parents.

She never did get a call back. Within three months Joanne's weight had dropped to ninety pounds and she had descended into a deep depression. She thought of suicide more often than she'd like to admit. But one thought kept her going—"If I survive," she told herself, "I'm going to make it so that no other woman has to go through what I did."

Two years after Cheyenne's death, Joanne founded the M.I.S.S. Foundation, an international organization now with more than seventy-five chapters around the world. Their website, www.missfoundation.org, receives more than 1.5 million hits a month. The M.I.S.S. organization provides practical resources and support for bereaved parents.

But it was not enough for Joanne to offer support to bereaved parents after the fact. She realized that she needed to provide physicians, nurses, medical examiners, and undertakers with resources to better care for parents in the midst of loss. "We're not going to make it a beautiful experience, but we can at least prevent additional trauma by training first responders to care more effectively," she says.

She went back to school and received her Master's in Social Work (MSW) and PhD, a doctorate in

Philosophy of Human Sciences so that she would have solid credentials to offer workshops to first responders. She's been teaching for eleven years and is amazed at the positive response to her workshops, which are consistently packed. What she's doing, after all, is ultimately quite simple—she's empowering medical professionals to care better, so that no bereaved mother has to fall through the cracks.

Jeannette Leavitt, mother of Andrew, who died just after his first birthday from meningitis, will never forget the compassionate care of the nurses and doctors who tended to Andrew during his final hours. They helped Jeannette and her husband, Steven, navigate the tangle of tubes and monitors so they could comfort Andrew during his final days in the hospital. They also showed them how to gently apply Vaseline to his chapped lips. Even after Andrew could no longer hear or see, his nurses and doctors approached him with loving awareness, "Hey, Buddy," they used to say as they entered his room.

There was one kind gesture, in particular, that Jeannette will never forget. When Andrew was prepared for the surgery that would remove his organs, Jeannette and Steve couldn't bear to stay. A nurse said, "I will stay with him for the surgery, and I will pray for him." Jeannette continues to draw comfort from the knowledge that the nurse stayed beside Andrew, offering him physical and spiritual support. "I don't even pray," Jeannette says, "but there is nothing she could have said that would have been more comforting to me than that."

While people sometimes experience wonderful, healing care from a loving community after miscarriage or infant death, others sometimes experience the opposite: demoralizing treatment that only increases the pain. When people receive loving care from a physical or spiritual community, the burden of their grief is shared by others—perhaps not lightened, but made more tolerable. Good care for the bereaved can have lasting effects, and these effects multiply again and again as those who experience good care reach out to others.

A Community of Care

Other couples express awe at the way they have been held by their communities—secular and religious. Jim Sparrow, who lives in a university community and is not formally connected to any religion, said that the death of his son Simon caused an awakening. As people poured into the local Unitarian Universalist church for Simon's memorial, Jim realized that more people loved his family—and his son—than he could have imagined. "I realized that there is this mostly invisible community during normal times that is connected to you morally and spiritually and that when a crisis occurs, you can finally see it."

Jim was amazed by the care of his community after Simon's death, as friends and neighbors filled their freezer with food and stepped in to care for their daughter, Elena. A group of moms from the community planted rose bushes in the Sparrows' back yard in honor of Simon. But perhaps the most powerful gestures of care came from those who called to share their own experiences with the death of a child.

"After Simon died, letters came in the mail and people poured out their hearts to us about their own experiences of the death of an infant or child," Jim says. "There are so many people out there who are walking around with loss."

Another couple, Father John and Jenny Hainsworth, are humbled by the care they experienced when their third child, Innocent, died through miscarriage. That week, Father John and Jenny were leading a summer camp for youth on a small Island near Vancouver Island, British Columbia. Jenny was just past her first trimester, and after two healthy pregnancies and births, she was not expecting anything to go awry. She had announced her pregnancy to friends and even written about it on her blog, and the church community they served was eagerly anticipating the birth.

When the cramping and spotting began, Father John and Jenny prayed together to the Virgin Mary, offering their child to her. They asked that if the child died, she would take the child back to God, and they said that if the baby were to survive, they would also dedicate the child to her.

The next day there was more bleeding, so Father John took Jenny to Vancouver Island so that she could receive care in a hospital. Jenny insisted that Father John return to the camp, telling him that everything would be fine. Following her direction, he returned.

Back at the camp, Father John received a call from Jenny with word that the baby had died. He was devastated by the news, but was in awe of the strength he heard in his wife's voice. "She was completed by God," he says. "She was held up by him."

Father John felt that some of her courage came from the camp community, which was praying for her. She called again and reported that she'd lost a lot of blood and the fetus had come out with it. She then had a D&C to remove all of the additional tissue. D&C stands for dilation and curettage—the procedure involves expanding the entrance of the uterus so that a thin metal instrument can scrape out all remaining fetal tissue. This procedure is done routinely when a doctor suspects an "incomplete miscarriage," meaning that some fetal tissue remains and could cause excessive bleeding or even a fatal condition for the mother.

That night, Father John couldn't sleep. He headed out to the small camp chapel at midnight. By candlelight, he offered prayers of supplication to the Mother of God. As he sang, "Most Holy Theotokos Have Mercy on Us," he turned around and realized that nearly thirty people had come into the chapel behind him to join him in prayer. He began to weep.

Later, he went to bed feeling exhausted. In the morning, he received a call that Jenny was ready to be picked up. He went to retrieve her, and when they got back to the camp he was amazed to see that she was well enough to teach her usual calligraphy class.

The couple was able to retrieve the remains of their child, which they named Innocent, after St. Innocent of Alaska. They chose this name because they loved the saint, and also because they did not know if the child was a boy or a girl. The name also seemed fitting because it reminded them of the term "Holy Innocents," which refers to the babies slain during King Herod's time.

They were invited to bury their child at a monastery. They headed there with their two children, Ella, who was five, and Heulwen, who was two. The children helped their parents sprinkle dirt on the casket. Father John was surprised at the way his children were able to cope with the miscarriage and integrate the knowledge of their sibling into their lives. They were not afraid to look at the baby's tiny body, or to see the small casket. Nor did they shrink back when asked to help sprinkle soil on the casket. It was as if they, like most adults, actually wanted something to do. To this day, if Ella is asked how many siblings she has, she'll say, "There's Heulwen, who is five, Innocent, who is dead, and Bridget Antigone, who is just a baby."

The Hainsworths' baby is buried just beside the cell of a monk they love, at his request. He wanted Innocent there so that he could look out each day and pray for the child. The monks refer to Innocent as one of their own.

The Ripple Effect

Quality care has a ripple effect—those who receive it often go on to extend the gift to others. They realize what is helpful and necessary, and how healing good care can be. They realize that for some, care is survival. Often, a couple who experiences the death of an infant will cause an awakening in their community—others will see that the pain is real and that this kind of thing can happen to anyone.

There is a definite ripple effect as love builds on love and people learn how to better care for others. After Father John and Jenny experienced their miscarriage, seven women in their small parish suffered miscarriages of their own over a fairly short period of time. "Because of our own experience, I've been able to reach out to these women in ways I never would have been able to before," Father John says. "We grieved so publicly, and I think that helped these women to know that they would not have to suffer without support." And as these women experienced their miscarriages, the parish community wept with them. There were not just seven miscarriages, hidden away and out of sight as these things often are, but there were seven burials as well—a public ritual to mark pain that is more often private.

Many parents describe a change in the way they relate to others after they experience the death of a child. While they may have wanted to run from the bereaved before, now they want to run to them, to help them know that they are not alone. The opening of the wound in your own life can make it impossible to ignore the pain in that of another.

Everly Macaro, mother of Simon, who died at sixteen months, remembers a friend whose baby died long before Simon did, of SIDS, or Sudden Infant Death Syndrome. SIDS is the sudden, unexplainable death of an infant between the ages of one month and one year. Everly remembers being shaken by the news of the baby's death, yet she did not know how to approach the family or what to say. Years later, she found herself calling that woman for help.

When she looks back on herself before the death of her son, she feels as if she was a completely different person, unfeeling, retreating from other people's pain. She remembers how a colleague's young daughter was run over by a truck. At the time, Everly's daughter Elena was just a year and a half. The news about her colleague made her feel nauseous and she couldn't bear to attend the service. "I just wanted to run away," she says.

Now, if she were to have a friend who experienced the death of a child, Everly says that she would want to call and check on them, to spend time with them, to say "I love you" over and over again. People said these words to her, even people who didn't know her well, and it helped. It made her think, "Wow, I am loved in a way I didn't know before."

Everly says that one of the consequences of experiencing the death of a child is that the experience is so surreal that you are taken out of the normal sphere of life. You're distracted, in a world of your own, and yet you long to integrate back into society in some way. At the same time you fear you might be shunned. "There are times when you just hope people aren't going to stop being your friend because you've experienced this unthinkable loss."

One of the most powerful ways to be a friend to a grieving parent is to be open to conversations about the child. Everly offers these words of advice to friends of bereaved parents: "Talk about the child. Ask the parents what they'll miss about him. When you lose a child you feel so alone. You need people to validate the enormity of the loss."

The death of Simon has also inspired Everly to learn everything she can about the strange and sudden illness that took him, MRSA. She's using her professional skills as a medical researcher and writer to try to crack the mysteries surrounding Simon's death. She's currently working with the pediatric infectious disease doctor who was responsible for Simon's autopsy. Dr. Robert Daum at the University of Chicago hospitals is an expert in MRSA. MRSA stands for Methicillin Resistant Staphylococcus Aureus bacteria. It is more commonly known as the "Superbug" and is a staph infection that is resistant to antibiotics and can be fatal. Dr. Robert Daum is currently overseeing a dozen studies on the disease.

Everly says that she "looks forward to having a better grip on where and how he contracted MRSA, what made him vulnerable in the first place, and how contagious the illness actually is." She feels that this work is just one more way to keep Simon's memory alive—and perhaps this research can help save the life of another child.

For many parents, reaching out to others is the beginning of healing. Helping others makes them feel less alone. The Zen Buddhist monk Thich Nhat Hanh says, "We are here to awaken from the illusion of our separateness." This is a necessary awakening, and the beginning of healing, not just for the other, but for the self as well.

Transformations

In *Year One: A Record*, John Tittensor experiences this type of awaking after the death of his child. Before he knew what it was like to grieve, he often turned away from grieving parents. Perhaps he couldn't bear to be present to their agony. But when he learns what it is like to suffer—to really suffer—he can never turn away again.

He writes:

> *The memory of my own response to this kind of loss before I became an initiate myself leaves me burning*

with shame and embarrassment. The friend I had not seen for years whose seven year old son was knocked down by a car and killed. The fellow teacher whose twin daughters died shortly after they were born. The cousin whose child simply died, inexplicably on its cot. Did I say anything? Send a message of consolation? Did I go to the funerals—as that cousin came to Jonathan's and Emma's? I look back on those days—not very long ago at all—with contempt and disgust and bafflement. So busy with my own preoccupations while knowing nothing of these most basic realities. I seem blind and without feeling, hardly human.

Yet there is a comfort. I have learnt something about what Martin Buber calls "living on the hard earth" and can at least hope that I am better for it. And one day I am going to face some poor, shattered human being and say,

"You can talk to me about it because I know exactly how you feel," and thus make up in some small way for the self-centeredness, the inexcusable insensitivity of the earlier uninitiated me.

Every parent I have known who has experienced the death of a child is profoundly changed by the experience. Many suffer from anxiety and depression afterward, and some say that grief was so all consuming at times that they feared they were poorer parents to their other children as a result. The loss of innocence that occurs after the death of an infant can also make parenting less enjoyable. One mother confessed that she felt that if she had not birthed a stillborn baby, she might have been able to be a better parent to her subsequent children—more attentive and confident.

While many parents express distress at negative changes in their lives as a result of infant loss, some also see positive changes. One of the most profound and common of these changes can be increased empathy and compassion for other bereaved people.

For many parents, the death of their infant became a catalyst in their lives that caused them to shift gears, to deepen and mature, both professionally and emotionally. Father Stephen Loposky, whose daughter died in his wife's womb shortly before she was born, believes that Kathryn's death had a profound effect on him: "Before I was priest, I was already fighting the battle to still hope and to love my daughter. Because I refuse to believe that Kathryn's death was the end for her, this resolve has made me fight tooth and nail when parishioners are leaning toward despair and senselessness."

Father Stephen remembers when he was first assigned to his parish, shortly after Kathryn had died. One of the first women he met was an eighty-year-old woman who had given birth to her only child—a stillborn baby—fifty-five years before.

She could not speak about the experience without crying. She described the agony of losing her own child as the woman who shared her room gave birth to her ninth child, a perfectly healthy baby that she didn't want. Father Stephen and this parishioner had a strong and immediate connection, and they remained close until she died at age eighty-eight. "She was the kindest person to children—she loved them all," he says.

The Gift of Tears

Like Father Stephen and his family, Jeannette Leavitt says that one of the results of her experience of Andrew's death is that if she hears of the death of another child, she can be completely devastated by it. She says that this change is sometimes incompatible with a healthy, productive life. She knows she loses a lot of time and energy weeping for others, which is somehow always connected to her own pain.

A wise person once told me: "A holy person always carries all persons inside of them." This saying reminds me of Jeannette, who would not describe herself as a religious person. Yet her willingness to bear the pain of others—or her inability to block it out—sets her apart as a uniquely compassionate person with a powerful capacity for love. While Jeannette sometimes finds her inability to block out the pain of others a burden, in many spiritual perspectives and traditions, such openness is seen as a gift.

Years ago I heard a man who works with men dying of AIDS speak about a profound moment in his spiritual journey. After walking with another man through his devastating descent into HIV and AIDS, and watching him die, this man threw himself on the ground weeping, asking God how he could allow the world to be filled with such pain. He felt, at the time, as if God said: "Now you know how I feel." And as this man thought again and again about what he learned through the experience, he says, "The more your heart is broken, the closer you are to the heart of God."

Tears are mentioned frequently in the scriptures as well. According to the Bible, God both stores all tears in a bottle (Ps. 56:8)—meaning he never, never forgets how many slipped down our faces—and promises to ultimately wipe them away (Is. 25:8). Not only that, but through Christ, God weeps and lets his own tears seep into our muddy world. Through this action, he says: *I feel it too, I ache as you do.*

In Eastern Orthodoxy one spiritual gift is emphasized above all others. It is the gift of tears. This gift is sometimes described as a mourning over your own sins and over all the world's aches. It is a real form of grief that opens the soul to receive joy. While the world we live in views tears as a sign of weakness and so often strives to avoid them, in the Christian tradition, tears have long been associated with intimacy with God, with wholeness, with a courageous and life-giving openness to the spiritual world.

Other Gifts

Cheryl Haggard's story is one of seeking the one thing she most needed after her son Maddux died, and trying to extend that gift to others. Before Maddux was born, her doctor warned her that babies born by C-section sometimes need time to recover. But Maddux struggled to breathe on his own. After a series of tests, it was thought that Maddux's cerebellum was underdeveloped. He did not have the capacity to breathe or move on his own. As Cheryl's doctor shared the devastating news with her, he said, "If a baby can't breathe, he can't live."

This news came as a devastating shock, because during the pregnancy multiple ultrasounds and an amniocentisis all had normal outcomes. During Maddux's short life, Cheryl and her husband had to walk many times through the maternity ward to get to the neonatal intensive unit, and she noticed that the walls in the maternity ward were lined with beautiful images of babies. "On the sixth day, my husband and I turned to each other and said, 'We want images of our son.'"

So her husband Mike contacted the photographer who had taken the hospital portraits, but the receptionist said that she wouldn't be available for a week. "That would be too late," Mike said. Something in his voice must have caught the receptionist off guard. She asked Mike to tell her a little more and he explained that his newborn son was going to die.

"Wait," the receptionist said, "let me get Sandy." The photographer got on the phone and promised to be there that evening. Cheryl's children came to the hospital and spent an hour with their younger brother. After they had left, Sandy did a photo session of Maddux with his parents. But Maddux was still in a tangle of tubes and the couple realized that those photos would never do their baby justice, so they asked if Sandy would come back after they'd removed life support so that Cheryl could have more organic images of her holding her son in the way she most desired—skin-on-skin.

After the first session, everyone stepped out of the room to allow Mike and Cheryl a few last moments with Maddux. They removed the life support and then invited Sandy back after Maddux had died. During the second photo session, Cheryl felt a little more at peace, but Mike felt very emotional, almost unable to cope with the presence of the photographer. Cheryl urged her husband to be in the photographs, because this would be his last chance to be in a photo with his son.

Maddux died on February 10, 2005. Leaving the hospital without their son was a surreal and agonizing experience for Mike and Cheryl. They were given a bag of items to take home—including mementos like a small teddy bear and a gold ring. But Cheryl didn't really know what to do with these items that had never touched her baby. "If I have any advice for hospital staff it would be to give these items to the parents before their baby dies so that they can put that little ring on the baby's finger, let the teddy bear nestle up to him, and then take these items that had actually touched their baby," Cheryl says.

The following weeks were devastating, "It was a pain I would not wish upon my worst enemy," according to Cheryl, "a pain that only death could take away—which was something I certainly wished for during that time." But during that bleak time, there was one ray of hope. "I knew that I had something good coming to me," Cheryl says, "because Sandy was working on those photos."

On February 25, Mike and Cheryl went to Sandy's studio. She put them in a room with a DVD player and set the slide show to play, accompanied by music. The couple watched the photos over and over. "I told Sandy she had given me my son back," Cheryl says.

For the next six months, Cheryl carried a portable DVD player around and played the video for anyone who wanted to see it. The images allowed her to feel more like a proud mother than a bereaved parent, although she was certainly both. "The response to that video was overwhelming," Cheryl says. "People loved it. And my former pastor asked for a copy to help as he counseled grieving families."

And then Sandy contacted Cheryl and began to put her in touch with other bereaved mothers. Sandy had a client who gave birth to a baby who was dying. Sandy had been asked to take photos, but the baby was connected to a gaggle of tubes and monitors. Sandy wanted her client to have the more natural, beautiful type of photos that Cheryl had, and yet she felt uncomfortable suggesting it. This birthed the question: "What if?" What if Cheryl could share her story about Maddux and Sandy could provide these "remembrance photographs" to grieving families? Sandy asked Cheryl to share her story with the client.

As this point, Sandy and Cheryl realized the need for these photo sessions was great. Together, they conceived of an idea—perhaps they could create a nonprofit organization to take memorial photographs of infants. Sandy could take photographs, and Cheryl could share her story. "As soon as we began to act on the idea, it was as if God said, 'Yes,'" Cheryl says. "Everything fell into our laps. A friend offered to help us get our 501c status, another helped with the brochure—everyone I knew seemed to have some reason they wanted to help us."

Now I Lay Me Down to Sleep, a nonprofit organization that takes portraits of babies that die after twenty-five weeks' gestation, now has a team of over five thousand professional volunteer photographers in nineteen different countries who are on call to take photographs of these babies. This past June, they finally hired an executive director.

Cheryl is grateful for the photographs and videos she has of Maddux, and she's grateful for the chance to help other parents all over the world. She offers this advice to grieving parents: "When you lose a baby, you're losing one of the greatest loves of your life. It's going to be painful. Surround yourself with people who want to hear your story and let yourself tell it."

For Cheryl, the death of her son has made her long to reach out in ways she might not have before.

She recently gave away a kidney to a friend in need, something she never would have done before. "After you lose a child, you discover that there are so many ways to reach out."

The opening of the wound is the beginning of awaking to the pain of others, and it is only through this process that we can realize that nothing is wasted; even heartache can be expansive if it increases our capacity to bear the pain of others. Remember those words from Thich Nhat Hanh: "We are here to awaken from the illusion of our separateness." This is a necessary awakening, and the beginning of healing, not just for the other, but for the self as well.

Suggestions for Parents
Who Want to Reach Out:

- Don't rush to do volunteer work before you're ready. Some parents told me that the urge was strong before they actually had the emotional resources. Plan to pace yourself and prepare to have less energy in the months ahead, as grief may sap much of your strength.
- If you are unsure of ways to reach out, reflect on your own experience and what was most helpful and what could have been better. When an opportunity arises, try to be the person you needed most during the most intense moments of your grief.

- Do what is most natural for you. Any skill can help another person—if you love to cook, prepare meals for those in need. If you love to knit, consider knitting tiny sweaters and blankets for premature babies. If you are a professional photographer, consider volunteering with Now I Lay Me Down to Sleep.

- If you take comfort in tending your child's grave, consider "adopting" the grave of another infant. You can leave flowers and teddy bears at the grave of any child, and unexpected kindness could bring healing to other parents.

- Many parents say that reaching out can be a lifeline during the worst times, when you are tempted to isolate and ruminate. Reaching out strengthens your connection to the child you love and transforms the world.

Suggestions for Bereaved Parents Needing Care:

- The news of your child's death will send ripples through your community. Be open to unexpected kindnesses from strangers and acquaintances, as well as to the possibility that some won't be able to engage your experience in a meaningful way.

- Don't be shy about asking for help. Those who offer are looking for something to do. Allow them to bring you a meal, take older siblings to school or on play dates, or help with cleaning and other life details.

- Honor those closest to you by giving them a role in the memorial service, even if it is as small as usher or arranger of flowers. For example, you might ask someone to select and arrange flowers or to purchase a book for friends and family to share thoughts and memories.

- Don't be afraid to gently tell others when their gestures of care are not helpful. When they say or do something that is not helpful, suggest alternatives.

- If you received care in a hospital that was not ideal, let your doctor and nurses know—otherwise their insensitive treatment will likely continue. Consider filling out a formal evaluation so that the hospital becomes aware of poor treatment of bereaved parents.

 *Marriage*

At first my father tried to have her relinquish the dead
infant to the nurse who spoke to my mother in soothing
words. He felt powerless as he sat there, staring straight
ahead, her body rigid, their child in her arms, rocking.
Rocking. Finally, allowing his grief to match hers, my
father knelt beside her, his arms around her and her
son, his body a shadow of her rocking motion.

And so my mother sat there for hours, her arms
around my brother, encircled by my father's arms.
From time to time the doctor entered the room, and
my father told him, "Not yet." By now he felt the
soothing rocking himself, felt the thread of his grief
woven into my mother's.

—from *"Floating in My Mother's Palm"* by Ursula Hegi

*A*n *Esquire* article from May 1996 describes a
"plot twist" that marks every marriage when
a dreadful event occurs. Either it will make the couple
become more inextricably bound together, or it will
turn lovers and companions into bitter strangers.

"Where you end up is not where you began, which
is both the heaven and the hell of marriage. You are
not who you were and she is not who she was, and the
balance on any given day, of whether that is a good or
bad thing, shifts precariously."

The author of the article goes on to describe the
transformative moment in her own marriage when

her husband stood up in a Washington church and preached a eulogy for his twelve-year-old son, sharing stories from his life and then asking the congregation to say his name out loud together, one last time:

> *My husband and I would never be the same after what happened to his son, the moment when I understood the horror and the beauty of the fact, the way in which we had been changed, the way in which our knowledge of each other was unfathomably deepened, the way in which we were inextricably a part of each other, was the moment that I finally felt that I knew what it was to be married.*

There is no question that many marriages falter in the aftermath of infant loss. Recent studies suggest that about one in four couples who experience the death of child will divorce as a result. The pressures are enormous and the response to death is varied and personal, sometimes making strangers of even the closest couples.

Even couples who grow closer through the experience face huge challenges and stress and they struggle to find space to grieve on their own terms while also trying to support the other. All couples encounter moments of decision—moments when they have to choose to try to see their spouse's point of view, moments when they struggle with the other person's response to the tragedy, moments when, if they are to survive as a couple, they have to accept things about their spouse that they didn't previously see or understand.

Jeanette and Steve, whose one-year-old son Andrew died of meningitis, survived this critical threshold and managed to grow stronger as a result. But Jeannette and her husband did not grieve in the same way. Especially when Andrew was dying in the hospital, Jeannette wondered why her husband wasn't as expressive as she was.

"He was quieter," she says. "He didn't cry all the time, like I did."

But then, one day, when Andrew was at the very end of his life, Steve and Jeannette went to the nearby Ronald McDonald House to take a shower. When Steve was in the shower, Jeannette heard him weeping. She then understood that his suffering was as great as her own, even if his tears did not always come out publicly.

During that first year after Andrew's death, Jeannette and Steve learned to work toward balance—they could each give the other space to grieve, and they could also support the other. By giving each other freedom, they were able to grow stronger together. "We realized early on that we're a team and we each needed to let the other grieve in the way that was most natural," Jeannette says.

Jeannette treasures an e-mail that Steve recently sent her while traveling, because it gave her a glimpse into his heart. He wrote about the experience of being at the airport when a mother received the remains of her son, a soldier killed in Iraq. In the e-mail, he wrote:

There was a U.S. Marine in full dress uniform . . .
carrying a metal box or plaque or something. . . . I
knew that they must be bringing the remains of the
dead soldier to the parents. It was a gray-haired lady
and her sister. It reminded me so much of walking out
of the hospital after we said goodbye to Andrew for
the last time. I can't stop thinking about the mom.

During the grieving process, couples often experience
not just one transformative moment, but many. One
grief is borne differently in two people, and men and
women may grieve in different ways. Although the grief
can feel as if it is breaking their marriage apart, many
couples can, with patience and love, work their way
through their differences.

Lyn and Rob also grieved differently and experienced
difficulties after their baby, Rebecca, died of Trisomy
18. After about a week, Rob went back to work and
Lyn was left home alone all day. Rob's life appeared to
return to normal as he assumed his old routine, but she
struggled with her long hours alone. For Lyn, it seemed
as if nothing would ever feel normal again.

"Now I was in my quiet house. I had no job, no family
nearby. I felt so alone," she says. "And then, when Rob
would come home from work, he didn't seem to want
to talk about Rebecca."

As the weeks passed, Lyn grew more and more
frustrated with Rob's silence surrounding their
daughter. She finally sat him down and told him what
was bothering her.

"Why don't you *ever* talk about her?" Lyn asked. "She's gone and you don't even mention her name. Have you forgotten her?"

"Of course not," Rob said. "I just can't bear to see you hurt so much."

At that point Lyn understood Rob's silence in a new way. And yet she wanted something other than silence from him. "I need you to begin to initiate the conversation," she said. "Then I won't feel so crazy all the time."

This conversation marked a turning point for Rob and Lyn. Although they continued to grieve in their own ways, Rob realized that he did not need to protect his wife with silence. More than silence, she needed to hear his words and thoughts and see his tears; she needed a sense that she was not alone.

For another couple—Jim and Everly Macario, whose one-year-old son, Simon, died of MRSA—growing closer through the experience only came after much struggle. "There were two marriages, actually," Jim says, "the marriage before we lost Simon and the marriage afterward."

Jim and Everly look back on their "first marriage" with the knowledge that they will never have that untroubled innocence again. And although they believe that bereaved parents and their children can be helped through therapy, for Everly and Jim, therapy sessions only seemed to aggravate unhealed wounds.

"Perhaps it was just too early," Jim says. "There is a time just to suture the wound, when trying to find some stability comes before all other concerns." Everly agrees, "The more therapy we had, the more we were at each other's throats."

But Everly and Jim did find their way through the struggles. "You have to get closer to get through it," Everly says. "You've got to try to lean on each other and also give each other space to grieve."

They helped each other find balance. "He's more of a manic person and I'm more of a depressive," Everly says. "Jim helped me because he is such a positive person. He tries not to take anything for granted and to count his blessings. Jim has a different perspective from me—he feels that we're lucky for every day we had with Simon, and that we were never entitled to him in the first place."

After Simon's death, Jim quickly realized that he could easily be consumed with bitterness, but he wanted to fight for a more balanced view of what had happened. "Obviously, I felt sad and angry that Simon wasn't able to stay with us longer—how wonderful it would have been to watch him grow up. But I didn't want to be bitter, because I felt that if I became bitter death would have won."

When Jim finally emerged from the shock and began to come to grips with what had happened, he found that he kept going back to certain memories for solace. He remembers holding Simon in the evening as he was putting Simon to sleep, the way that Simon would nestle his head into Jim's shoulder. "I would look out of Simon's bedroom window and think to myself, 'I've got to savor this. I will never have this again.'"

In retrospect, Jim doesn't really understand why he thought that way at that time. They could not have guessed that their hearty, healthy son would die from a sudden illness. But Jim is grateful for all those moments when he was able to grasp that Simon's presence in their life was a precious gift, moments when he was able to slow down and cherish him.

And Jim is also grateful that Simon was with his mother just before he lost consciousness. "During World War I, when soldiers were dying on the battlefield, their number one request was 'Mama.' And for a baby, their mother is the whole world. I was grateful that Everly was with Simon as he said his last word, which was 'Agua.' He wanted water, and Everly was there to give it to him."

New Levels of Tenderness

Stephanos and Juliana, whose son Philip died at twelve and a half weeks' gestation, say that they had some very rocky moments in the first week, when they discovered how differently they responded to what had happened and as they struggled to process feelings of guilt and blame.

Like many of the couples I spoke to, they went through a period of wracking their brains trying to figure out why this had happened. Had they done something wrong? Were they cursed? Even as they struggled over these questions, they eventually came to realize that these thoughts weren't productive. They were also comforted by a consultation with a maternal care specialist who reviewed their case and determined that the miscarriage occurred because of placental abruption and could not have been prevented.

But even as they began to let go of the guilt, the pain remained. For Stephanos, one of the hidden agonies of losing his first son was that he had just begun to feel like a father—the very idea of the child growing in his wife's womb was changing him, both internally and externally. He began to drive more slowly and cautiously, and he began to think not just in terms of caring for his wife, but also of caring for the child. "With fatherhood, there came this awesome sense of responsibility. It was amazing how it was changing me and I was growing into it and anticipating it," he says.

Stephanos and Juliana were traveling in separate cities when Stephanos got word that Juliana was bleeding. His feeling of awesome responsibility became a feeling of helplessness and frustration as he realized what was happening and that he was powerless to change it. He turned questions around and around in his mind as he struggled with his role in the miscarriage: Did I let her get too stressed? Was I loving enough? Did I pray hard enough?

As the couple grieved and struggled over these unanswerable questions, Stephanos realized that he would never be the same, that the idea of their child growing in his wife's womb had transformed him. "I had no idea that this tenderness was in me, it exposed new heights and depths in my heart."

Even as the couple had begun to change because of the knowledge that they were going to become parents, they suddenly had to change again as they encountered the storm of grief that swept through their marriage, tossing over all the chairs, shattering the windows, blowing the doors open, reshaping them as individuals and as a couple.

After Philip's death, Stephanos spent lots of time alone at his grave, praying. He pushed most of his regular responsibilities to the back burner so he could process what had happened. Juliana also needed projects to keep her busy and her mind occupied, but the things that were most helpful for Stephanos, such as visiting Philip's grave, were often traumatic for her, causing disturbing dreams and reopening wounds that were just barely beginning to heal. Juliana threw herself into creative work—she made a scrapbook about Philip and a CD of songs that reminded her of him. She felt as if she was always crying, even as she wrote poetry and began work on an icon of St. Philip.

After they navigated the tensions of that first week, Stephanos and Juliana found that they were able to feel close to each other, despite their different ways of grieving. And ultimately, their grief brought them closer. They did not have to grieve in the same way—or in the same moments—to feel is if they were together.

During the writing of this book, Juliana gave birth to their second child, a boy, named Hariton, "Harry." The process of preparing for their second child stirred up grief for both of them, especially when they were setting up the nursery. Both found that they had to stop now and then just to let the tears come. They knew that it should have been Philip's room first. Like many couples today who have gone through miscarriage or experienced the death of an infant, when they announced their pregnancy and Harry's birth, they cautioned friends and family not to assume that the new pregnancy undid the pain of the death of their first son. And while Stephanos and Juliana have found that the grief has become a little less intense, it hasn't left them. It's never too far from the surface.

Stephanos offers this advice to husbands in his situation: "Don't ask why. Don't blame. Try with all your life to trust God and to hold your wife, to comfort and caress her, to lose yourself in taking care of her."

Both Stephanos and Juliana are grateful for the way they were able to come together in spite of the grief— or perhaps because of it. "We grew together and grew stronger in the way that a fractured bone can repair itself with time," Stephanos says.

Couples who have experienced this kind of grief know that it lingers for many years as they turn their experience over and over again, retracing their steps, trying to understand what went wrong.

Father Stephen and Daria, whose first child, Kathryn, died just before labor, have struggled ever since to fit together the pieces of the puzzle. "I can't tell you how many times we had the same conversation," Father Stephen says. "She would ask me, 'Why is God punishing us like this? God doesn't love us, He's not watching over us.' She always felt that she was to blame. She felt that she should have known something was wrong. There were times when I felt absolutely helpless—incapable of helping and supporting her, times when I just couldn't get through."

But for them, the death of a child early in their marriage forced them to grow up and to grow close. "This need not be something that separates you. It can actually draw you closer together if you can support each other but each give the other space to grieve," Father Stephen says.

The couple remembers the surreal experience of selecting Kathryn's casket. "How do you pick out a baby's casket?" Father Stephen asks. There were two baby caskets to choose from—one that looked like a miniature adult casket and another that had a strange white woolly top. They selected the one with the fluffy top and then covered it with a cloth that had been used in their wedding ceremony. "That helped bind us—and the two sacraments—marriage and that of burial—together," Father Stephen says.

They also remember the long drive from the funeral to the cemetery with Kathryn in the casket in the back seat. Father Stephen says that trip gave them some space after the crowded funeral service. "After Kathryn's death, we did question and doubt, but that particular trip was peaceful. We renewed our energy and commitment."

But one of their most vivid memories is the long walk that they took from the car to their apartment when they were returning from the hospital without Kathryn. "The hardest steps I've ever taken, as a man, a husband and a father, were the fifty paces from our car to our apartment without Kathryn," Father Stephen says. "I didn't think we were ever going to get there. Daria leaned on my shoulder, and I leaned on hers, and it felt like an eternity. I'll never forget those steps we had to take together. But I was grateful that it was her I was leaning on."

Relationship Suggestions for Bereaved Couples:

- As questions of guilt and blame emerge, seek a same-sex friend to confide in, as these thoughts are not helpful for your spouse to hear.
- People not only grieve differently, but they often grieve on different timelines. If you want to be present with your partner in his or her grief, allow your partner to let his or her grief surface in its own time and form.

- It may be helpful to speak to a counselor. If you find that these meetings only stir up more tension, however, consider postponing counseling to a later time.
- Try not to isolate yourself. If possible, reach out to another couple that has experienced the death of a child.
- If you or your spouse consumes excessive alcohol, drugs, or food to cope with the pain, consider getting help. Addiction ultimately isolates and destroys.
- If you begin to think about separating, know that grief stirs up extreme emotions. Give yourself time to untangle your feelings about the death of your baby from your feelings about your spouse.

 *Signs*

*Enter each day with the expectation that the happenings
of the day may contain a clandestine message addressed
to you personally. Expect omens, epiphanies, casual
blessing, and teachers who unknowingly speak to your
condition.*

—Sam Keen

*Y*ears ago, I visited some friends after their baby
died at three months from trisomy 18, a rare
genetic disorder. Also called Edwards syndrome, named
for the geneticist who first identified the disorder,
trisomy 18 afflicts about one in every six thousand live
births and is nearly always fatal within the first year.

On a dreary day in Vancouver, British Columbia, my
friends took me to the cemetery to see where their son
was buried. As we walked toward the grave, a rainbow
arched over the mound of fresh dirt. My friend is Polish
Orthodox, her husband a Moroccan Muslim. None of
us needed words to convey that we all heard the same
message coming through that glorious rainbow.

The more stories I hear about the death of infants, the
more convinced I am that there are certain patterns that
often accompany them. These are not necessarily rigid
rules about how things will unfold in every situation,
but are commonalities between stories that are
impossible to write off as coincidences. This is certainly
the case with the phenomenon of signs, which is more

widespread and universal that I initially imagined. Perhaps the intensity of tragedy forces God to up the ante, to be a catalyst for events that are mysteriously good and beautiful, that will stand out in sharp relief against the backdrop of devastation.

In all the stories in this book, the first miracle that the parents hoped for did not occur—the child did not survive, was not healed, did not recover. But sometimes there were other miracles. Among the debris of all the seemingly unanswered prayers, there is sometimes a shimmer of hope.

Almost every story contains an unexpected stroke of grace, a sign that the child is either under the mercy of God or mysteriously, continuously at work in the parents' lives. While outsiders might be skeptical of such signs, these occurrences offer tremendous comfort to parents in the midst of their grief. And even initially skeptical parents often begin to trust what they see and experience, choosing to accept the comfort and joy that comes through these unusual events.

Jeanette and Steve's son, Andrew, died when he was just over one year in age, of meningitis. To this day, Jeanette offers this advice to parents who have suffered the death of a child: "Be open to signs." If you were to meet Jeanette, you would understand why her advice caught me off guard at first. She's articulate, intelligent, practical, and not particularly religious. And yet, for her and Steve, the months after Andrew's death were rife not only with agonizing grief, but also with seemingly random moments of presence, with a sense that Andrew was mysteriously at work in their lives, helping them as they struggled to move forward.

Andrew's liver was donated to a three-month-old baby girl who had been given just two weeks to live. Shortly after Andrew died, just before Christmas, Jeanette and Steve received a letter from the parents of this little girl, Emma. Emma's parents told Steve and Jeanette that they would like to meet them and thank them in person, and that they would like them to know their daughter, who was alive and healthy because of Andrew's gift.

The couples arranged to meet on Mother's Day that year. Steve and Jeannette wanted to bring a gift for Emma, something that Andrew owned, so that she could know him a little bit better. They finally settled on his beloved Winnie the Pooh Bear.

When they first met Emma, she was wearing a Winnie the Pooh outfit. She also loved Winnie the Pooh! Not only that, but she was a joyful, smiling child, much like Andrew. But perhaps the greatest surprise that day was one of Emma's special gestures—she would raise both arms up in the air as her parents said, "Touchdown!" This had been one of Andrew's favorite games as well.

In an e-mail to Emma's parents, Jeanette described their experience of meeting Emma:

> *Emma has also given something very special to us. She's keeping part of Andrew alive. She's allowing us*

to know that there's a part of him—an actual living,
physical part of him—that lives on and will grow
inside of your little girl. Even though we know that
Andrew's spirit will always live and be with us, we feel
like Emma is also carrying some of Andrew's spirit,
and that makes us happy.

For Jeannette and Steve, the experience of meeting
Emma was one of the strange graces of that first
difficult year without him. As Jeannette wrote in her
letter to Emma's parents after that first meeting, "What
a crazy, strange, sad, painful, and yet wonderful and
special connection we have." It was Andrew, after all,
that had brought them together, and it is Andrew, even
now, who has made family from strangers—knitting
their fates inextricably together.

Another experience that stands out for Jeannette
occurred just after they'd attended their first grief
support group with an organization called The
Compassionate Friends. Andrew had a little onesie that
read "Little Stinker," and they used to affectionately
call him that. On their way home from that last
meeting, they were thinking of Andrew's nickname
and playfully decided to look for a skunk along the
highway.

Within ten seconds, they spotted a living baby skunk,
hanging out by the side of the road. "How often does
one see a skunk in Chicago?" Jeanette asked. They
couldn't believe their eyes, so they looped around and

drove past the skunk one more time. It was just waiting there, as if it had been expecting them. Since that day, they've never seen another skunk in Chicago.

Simon's Flowers and Birds

Jim Sparrow once told me about an experience that broke his heart and astonished him on his son Simon's last day. Jim took Simon to the emergency room on a Friday morning after the child woke with an unearthly, primal scream and fever. About an hour later, Everly joined Jim, and she remembers the way Simon was sleeping on her husband's lap. "I will never forget how angelic Simon looked . . . the reddish tint from his blondish/brownish hair glowed in such a way that it made me think that there was a halo surrounding his beautiful, cherub-like face," Everly wrote after Simon's death. "He seemed so peaceful and content in his daddy's lap; I felt relieved."

At that point, doctors were unable to correctly diagnose Simon with MRSA, the acronym for a bacterium that causes aggressive infections in human beings. The doctors initially suspected that he was asthmatic because of his labored breathing, and prescribed an Albuterol inhaler. After several hours at the emergency room, he was released around noon.

Jim left the hospital, with Andrew limp against his shoulder. But as they passed some bushes, Andrew looked down and spotted one of the first buds of spring. Then he said a word that he had never said before;

distinctly, clearly, he said, "Flower." "It was a red-orange blur, a small bud just pushing up, surrounded by the usual grey-brown leaves and dead vegetation that predominate in winter time," Jim says.

Flower was the last word that Jim ever heard his son say. "He said it in such a feeble, faraway voice," Jim says. "It really worried me." When Jim strapped Simon into his car seat, his son—who usually wriggled as he was being strapped in, was unusually compliant. "He was limp as a noodle," Jim says, "and it scared me."

But Jim thought his concerns must have been out of touch with reality, because he'd already returned once to the emergency room. As they stepped out of the hospital, they noticed that Simon's lips were blue. They turned around and took him back to the doctor. "His lips are blue," Jim said. "There's got to be something wrong."

So the doctor hooked Simon up to a monitor. Jim could see that his son was getting enough oxygen, so he decided he was probably overreacting and that everything would be okay. Jim was slated to give a lecture a few hours away that day and he asked the doctor if he should move forward as planned. "Do whatever you would normally do," the doctor suggested.

And so this time, even though Jim had a gnawing feeling that something was seriously wrong with Simon, it also seemed possible that he might be overreacting. He said to himself, "Other people don't blow off their professional commitments just because their kids get sick." And he decided to drive to his lecture.

Back at home, things took a turn for the worse. Simon vomited the small amount of milk he'd had that morning and he lay limply in Everly's arms. His lethargy really concerned Everly, as Simon was usually an active child. He also kept asking for "agua," the word for "water" in Spanish, and drank four sippy cups full of water, only to vomit it all up.

Everly knew something was seriously wrong when Simon's cheeks and forehead were cold and his lips began to turn blue again. "His nostrils were also flaring and his chest was expanding and contracting in the shape of a barrel. At about 4:30 p.m., I called the doctor to have her listen to Simon's labored breathing and she said, 'Hang up and call 911.'"

About a minute after Everly called 911, Jim called home to check on her and got the news that an ambulance was on the way. This time at the hospital, something dramatic had shifted in Simon and in the way the physicians dealt with him. Everly was so frantic that the only thing she could think of to do was to call her parents. She had to leave Simon briefly to make that call. When she returned, she found out that Simon had been taken to the pediatric intensive care unit.

"I was escorted to the Pediatric ICU, where Simon was connected to what seemed like a hundred tubes, still with his eyes open and looking around," Everly says. "The doctors kept repeating, 'Your child is very, very sick. Your child is very, very sick.' I caressed

Simon's curly hair, from his part over to his side, near his ear, and responded, 'His eyes are open. Isn't that a good sign?' I knew something was seriously wrong by the expression on the doctors' faces. They seemed confused, scared, frantic and helpless themselves."

At this point, Everly was brought into a conference room where she was told that Simon had an infection, with the source and specific diagnosis yet unknown. It was only through Simon's autopsy that MRSA—an illness that neither Jim nor Everly had ever heard of— was finally diagnosed.

While Everly was in the pediatric ICU with Simon, Jim was driving back to be with his son and wife. "I think the worst part for me was that long trip back, alone in the car, knowing something was horribly wrong with my son," Jim says.

By the time Jim returned to the hospital, Simon had lost consciousness. Jim describes that night as "a dark night of the soul." Everly felt that Simon had left them at about ten p.m. that night, although Simon's death certificate says he died the following day, at noon.

That night, as the MRSA took Simon, a terrible downpour flooded the streets of Chicago. After the torrential downpour that night, the weather the following morning only added to Jim and Everly's surreal agony. Jim says, "The next morning, he lingered near death for some hours, and the sun was already clear and bright, streaming through the ER windows in what I consciously recognized as a cruel irony. After he died, Everly and I walked out into a brilliant, almost painfully sharp, clear spring day." And this is when a sign hit them like a ton of bricks: "It seemed that all the flowers had suddenly begun to blossom!" Simon's flower had become a multitude.

"It really did feel like the first day of spring, as if the previous day had taken place weeks or months before. There was a boy playing with a ball in the sun, on the brick. It was all too vivid and detached from what we had just been through, as if we had passed into another world that just happened to resemble the one we'd left the day before," Jim says.

The days that followed were marked by strange weather patterns. Tornadoes touched down and wind whipped through the city for days, so powerful that it slammed doors and knocked things down and made the rocker on Jim and Everly's front porch sway back and forth. Friends staying with them commented on the strange weather.

Jim and Everly both felt that there was a message for them in the eerie weather. "I felt like Simon had gone out into nature and was touching us through it," Jim says. Their world had been turned upside down and torn apart; the fierce wind and tornado touchdowns seemed oddly fitting.

Jim recognizes that the signs and unusual experiences surrounding Simon's death could simply be wish fulfillment. He understands that many people will think these things about them. But he was still willing to take comfort in whatever form it came, particularly during those desperate days after Simon's death.

Jim is not quite sure where he picked up this idea, but after Simon's death, he had a vague notion that sometimes the soul of the departed comforts the bereaved through the presence of birds. A few months after Simon's death, he and Everly were again in downtown Chicago, by Lake Michigan at Navy Pier. It was still cold and wintry, and there were no animals around. Suddenly, Jim heard a cardinal. "It was such a trill, singular song," Jim says. "And then I saw it—it was brilliant red, standing on a windowsill with a drab Chicago day behind it. And it was looking directly at me."

A few months after Simon's death, the family was walking together again and an oriel with a bright orange chest landed just beside Everly's foot. Then, on the one-year anniversary of Simon's death, a bright red oriel flew up to Jim and gazed at him for a long, quiet moment. He looked back at the bird with wonder.

These experiences have caused Jim to reflect on his Catholic upbringing. While he is no longer affiliated with any institutional religion, he says that one interpretation of the experience is that God's grace was coming from Simon's soul through the birds, so that the family wouldn't feel so desolate.

He realizes now that before having children he might have disregarded these kinds of experiences. Perhaps he wouldn't have even seen the birds or noticed the flowers. But his children opened him to a new way of seeing and living in the world. "I was given another life, another youth, through my children," he says, "and that is really a precious gift."

Trusting Your Intuition and Dreams

In Joanne Cacciatore's book *Dear Cheyenne*, she describes an unusual encounter that occurred a few months after Cheyenne's death. During those first months, she often went to the cemetery to tend Cheyenne's grave. Putting flowers on the grave was one of her few comforts during that time, one way she could be with Cheyenne and feel that she was still taking care of her.

When she visited Cheyenne's grave she found that she was also drawn toward another, that of a little boy named Timothy James, nicknamed "Peter Pan" according to his gravestone. She spent a lot of time tending his grave as well. One day she left a teddy bear there. That day, she told her husband that one day she'd like to meet Timothy's mother.

The next day, she attended a Compassionate Friends meeting. Parents brought pictures of their children. Joanne was drawn to the photo of a sweet, blond-haired boy. She stared at it for a long time. As the parents shared their stories, one mother spoke about her two-year-old son who had died of no clear cause. As she spoke, Joanne realized that this was Timothy's mom! This woman confirmed Joanne's intuition when she claimed that photo of the sweet blond boy as her own.

"Thinking my imagination had gone wild, I asked her where he was buried. I was right! She was the one I had wanted to meet," Joanne writes. "I told her I was the one who had been leaving things at his grave. We hugged each other and cried. She told me that I helped her immensely. She felt such joy that someone else cared enough to leave things at his grave and care for his sacred burial place."

Anne Morrow Lindbergh, author of *Gifts from the Sea* and wife of the famed pilot Charles Lindbergh, experienced the death of their young son, Charles Jr. In her journals, she wrote from the raw place of grief. She describes dreams of horror and dreams of consolation. She writes about a dream in which her son was condemned to die and she was raging at the people who would ultimately take his life. She also writes about a delicious sleep in which she'd encounter Charles Jr.:

> *Englewood, Tuesday, June 9, 1932:*
> *I wake each morning (even when I do not dream) with a vague feeling that I have been close to the baby all night. I go to bed thinking of him—so vividly I almost see him—and then continue unconsciously in sleep. It is good, for by day he is getting further and further away—even the clothes . . . I have looked at them three or four times, have lost his presence.*

Sometimes siblings also experience comforting dreams after death occurs. Rachelle Mee-Chapman's daughter Eden, who was born a year after her brother Simeon died, experienced the death of her grandfather, "Buddy." After he died, she told her father, "Daddy, I saw Buddy and Simeon in heaven together and they were playing football!" According to Rachelle, her husband burst into tears. "He was convinced that Eden had a connection with Simeon that allowed her to break through and see something we could not."

Lyn, mother of Rebecca, also had a dream of comfort a few months after Becca died. That night she had cried herself to sleep, only to wake feeling serene the following morning. In her dream, she saw Rebecca, not much older that two, running through a field. Becca was telling Jesus about her day, and the whole dream was infused with bright light. "On this earth, her body was not just fragile, but broken," Lyn says. "There is no other place she could be perfect but in her Father's arms."

Embracing the Mystery

There is a possibility that the ties to deceased children—and between siblings—remain strong long after death has occurred, and that even as the years wear on, unusual encounters can occur. My neighbor, a pastor, recently returned from Chile, where he attended his sister's funeral. Everything about her death had been tragic—she was a nurse, walking down a snowy mountain on a cold night to get to the hospital for her shift, when she began to vomit. She had a pancreatic condition that must have caused the vomiting to intensify, and she eventually passed out in the snow beside a dark road. There, she froze to death.

But my neighbor told me that something unusual occurred that night. A friend of the family had been driving on that snowy road late that night. She had seen a child playing by herself by the side of the road in exactly the spot where his sister had died. It was a strange sight at that hour and in that weather, and later on, the woman agonized over the fact that she did not stop.

"But my sister was a twin," he told me. "Her twin died when she was a toddler." I asked him if he thought that perhaps the twin had come to help his sister over the threshold. He just shook his head at me, smiling sadly, "That," he said, "is a mystery."

Suggestions Related to Signs:

- Keep in mind that although parents often experience signs and dreams they can remember, this does not occur in every case. It is wise to be open to signs, but not to seek or expect them.

- Keep a journal of your experiences after your child's death. Although you may think that your memories will never fade, many do, and you may need to go back to certain dreams or experiences for comfort. If you have a good dream, write it down as soon as you wake, even if you wake in the middle of the night. The record will be worth the lost sleep later on!

- If friends and family are skeptical of your experiences, don't let their responses mitigate your joy. Some people are not able to accept things they cannot understand with their rational minds.

- Seek out friends who value your experiences and insights and let the conversation grow with time.

- If one of your children has a dream or experience that brings comfort, encourage them to draw a picture of what they saw or write it down if they are able.

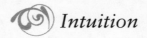 *Intuition*

> *The intuitive mind is a sacred gift and the rational mind a faithful servant. We have created a society that honors the servant and has forgotten the gift.*
>
> —ALBERT EINSTEIN

*D*r. Victor Shamas, a psychology professor at the University of Arizona, recently conducted a study of maternal intuition during pregnancy. He was interested in discovering if pregnant women were able to correctly intuit the sex of their children in utero.

Seventy percent of the women he studied were able to predict—or intuit—the sex of their babies. He found that, in most cases, when a woman was unable to predict the sex of her child, the factor that interfered was maternal desire—a mother who strongly preferred one sex over the other was less likely to be able to accurately read her intuition.

Dr. Shamas was not entirely shocked by these findings, but the greatest surprise came to him after the study was complete and released to his academic colleagues. He was disturbed to hear that the findings were routinely dismissed by other academics. "But by the standards of modern psychological research, 70 percent is huge. There are researchers who have received international acclaim for research that has produced much smaller effects than these," Dr. Shamas says.

Dr. Shamas believes that the main reason this study has been marginalized is because intuition cannot be quantified. "It does not fit within the existing paradigm in psychology and neuroscience. At this time, we have no way of explaining how a mother can detect the sex of her unborn baby or predict a future event in that child's life. And yet it makes no sense to reject something simply because we have not yet come up with an explanation for it."

Dr. Shamas's studies go beyond sex prediction. He has discovered through his research that pregnant mothers often have intuition about several aspects of the pregnancy and health of their unborn child. "Women who experience a miscarriage or stillbirth often have a premonition related to complications in the pregnancy, and these premonitions tend to occur long before there are any detectable signs of a problem," he says.

Because of his findings, Dr. Shamas believes that physicians should not ignore intuition in pregnant women. "If I were advising medical professionals involved in prenatal care, I would urge them to pay close attention to a mother who expresses these types of concerns. Even if a large percentage of such cases turn out to be the unfounded fears of an anxious mother, there are enough cases in which the mother is right to merit extra attention on the part of the provider."

Dr. Shamas believes that intuition plays a far more powerful, and potentially helpful, role in our lives than people realize. "We may not know exactly how it works, but people who rely on their intuition on a daily basis—and I am one of those people—know beyond a shadow of a doubt that it works. In fact, I would say that intuition is one of the most powerful tools that we have at our disposal."

Dr. Shamas's research findings certainly resonate with many mothers who describe strong feelings during their pregnancies or afterward that something was just not right. In fact, many of the parents who experience miscarriage or the death of a young infant have a great deal of intuition about the baby during the pregnancy and during and after the baby's death. Many mothers raise concerns with their doctors and are told not to worry. But no matter how hard they try to think "reasonably" about the situation, the concerns keep rising to the surface.

At times, a parent's intuition may be clouded by his or her own desire for a healthy child. But intuition before, during, and after the death of an infant is a gift to parents, one that should be valued and respected.

Listening to God

Intuition is something that we know by direct apprehension—there is no reason involved, no physical hearing, just an awareness that can grow, with time, into a certainty. The intuitive experience is a fundamentally human one, not limited to any particular religious expression. Intuition, it seems, is an equal opportunity employer.

Historically, many of the great Christian saints had experiences that we might call intuitive. They heard voices that nobody else heard. They "recognized" people they'd never met on this earth. Just as Jesus "knew" things about the woman at the well, many Christian saints could see into the souls of those they came into contact with.

That said, within Christianity there seems to be both an openness to intuition and a caution to find the proper balance. Within most traditions, the expectation is that intuition is understood and interpreted in context and community. If something is true, then it seems fitting that it will resonate in the hearts of more than one person—that confirmation can be found in community.

Many Christians speak of profound experiences with special people—monks or nuns, priests or ministers, a special counselor or perhaps a spiritual director—who seem to have a gift of being able to see into their hearts, to recognize and articulate their secret struggles in a way that is ultimately healing. This kind of knowledge is a spiritual gift that is given by God—not sought after or somehow earned—and received freely when it comes.

I believe that it is possible to hear God, to know things about our own lives and those we love. But I am also cautious—I always try to check my perceptions against people I trust. As the dean from the seminary I attended used to say, "Every day you should admit to yourself that you could be wrong." So I try to strike a balance between the two: I try to follow the still small voice of God wherever it leads me; but I am also willing to make a U-turn when I check my perceptions against reality and the two don't line up.

Visions and Impressions

Cheryl Haggard, mother of Maddux, who died soon after birth, told me that during her pregnancy she had two experiences that were outside of the norm and did not cohere with her prenatal screenings. According to her ultrasounds and amniocentesis, everything was progressing normally. But for Cheryl, who was in her fourth pregnancy, something didn't feel quite right. Maddux didn't move like her other kids had—she could feel gentle nudges at times, but she never felt the strong kicks that were the norm in her other pregnancies. When she mentioned this to her doctor, he told her that the screenings didn't suggest any reason for alarm. And of course, medically speaking, he was probably right, but Cheryl's intuition said something else.

Cheryl had experienced a vision and a dream. Both were troubling, but she decided to chalk them up to her overactive imagination. The vision occurred when she was setting up the nursery for Maddux. When the nursery was finally in order, as she stood in his room, she suddenly saw an image of a baby covered in tubes and cords. She said to herself, "Maddux will never be in this nursery." It was a frightening sight, and one that Cheryl chose to ignore at the time. Because she had already had three healthy pregnancies and because none of the prenatal tests had come in as abnormal, it seemed silly to be overly alarmed.

But there was also one unusual dream during the pregnancy—a dream that remains vivid for Cheryl to this day. She had nursed each of her previous babies in the middle of the night in a rocker in her bedroom. In this dream, Cheryl was up with Maddux to nurse. She was watching television and not paying too much attention to Maddux, and he was struggling to latch on. Suddenly, she looked down and saw that her arms were empty. There was no Maddux.

During the pregnancy she also had a strong feeling that she should do things in a certain way, and she followed her intuition in these things, sensing that her feelings were leading her in the way she needed to go. For example, when it was discovered that Maddux was breech, she chose to have a C-section rather than have the doctors try to turn him. She now feels grateful for her insistence on the C-section, as she fears that he might not have survived that kind of manipulation or the vaginal birth.

Each step of the way, Cheryl felt that she was being nudged by her intuition to do things in a particular way. Although Maddux died shortly after he was born, she feels that her intuition helped her to make choices that allowed him to be born alive, which was a gift in itself. No prenatal screening was able to give the knowledge that welled up irresistibly in Cheryl's heart: that Maddux was fragile and needed special care every step of the way.

Intuition can also play a powerful and helpful role for parents attempting to navigate a situation they've never faced before—the death of a baby. In Martha Beck's *Expecting Adam*, she recounts a story from when her son Adam was two years old. She found him face down in the bathtub, limp and unconscious. She gave him CPR with no prior knowledge of what to do. She writes: "The silent voice that had alerted me to the danger in the first place began to give me quick, clear instructions. My body followed with an eerie calm as though it was under the control of someone far more self-assured. I put Adam down on his back, blew air into his nose and mouth, then turned his head and pressed gently on his sternum. After five or six repetitions of this procedure, a gush of water bubbled out of Adam's lungs and he drew a shallow breath."

Intuition is available to all who are willing to quiet themselves enough to hear that still, small, persistent voice that often comes back again and again until we receive the message. It often takes a while for us to hear because we aren't used to listening in this way. Most of us are half blind and half deaf. But listening is an ancient and valuable practice, and we can get better at it with time.

For the Christian, this quietness comes through prayer, through a willingness to carve out a little more space each day for the Holy Spirit, which increases our capacity to bear and reflect love. That's what authentic intuition is ultimately about: love. Love is the source and softening, the gentle knock at the door, the flood of light we step into as we face the unthinkable.

Suggestions Related to Intuition:

- According to Dr. Victor Shamas, it may be natural for parents to worry about their children, but intuition is different from fear. "These signals come from a much deeper place, and they tend to have a force and clarity that are unmistakable."
- If you share your concerns with your doctor and your doctor is not responsive enough, be persistent. Don't hesitate to ask for a second opinion or switch physicians entirely. (Sometimes this will have cost implications, as health insurance plans can be limiting, but you'll be glad you were persistent, in the long run.)
- Make a scene if you need to. Victor Shamas writes, "Scream and shout: righteous indignation commands attention. Demand action at all cost. In this case, the only reasons for hesitation are self-doubt or shame. Become selfless and shameless in pursuit of your child's well-being."
- Surround yourself with people who respect you enough to hear you out even when your concerns are based on a hunch or your faith that God is leading you to some understanding. Surround

yourself with friends who strengthen your faith. Supportive friends and family will help build your confidence should you need to advocate for yourself or your child in a medical crisis.

 *The Other Child*

Why can't they understand?
If I become blind
In one of my eyes,
Of course I am still grateful
For the vision that remains in the other.

But I will never stop mourning the absence of
My precious eye
The one which I lost.

My vision has changed forever.
I will never, ever
See things the same way again.

—JOANNE CACCIATORE

A few months after Hurricane Katrina devastated New Orleans in 2005, National Public Radio's news program *All Things Considered* ran a story about the way that the trees responded to the disaster. They featured Joe and Lucianne Carmichael, who own seven acres of bottomland hardwood forest—the last patch of such foliage in all of Orleans Parish.

When the couple heard that Katrina was coming, they packed up and headed out, only to return forty-one days later, at the soft edge of autumn, to a mess of fallen trees and debris. But there was something unusual about the disheveled forest: a magnolia tree—a tree that is only supposed to bloom in spring—was covered in white shell petals.

According to their groundskeeper, those trees were doing exactly what they needed to do—creating a rush of seeds in autumn, when they would normally be dropping leaves and preparing for sleep, so that new trees could root among the fallen. They had plunged into reproductive overdrive as a matter of survival.

Even the trees seem to understand that catastrophe calls for a unique and courageous response, a sewing of the torn seams of life together with fresh possibility. As Michele Norris wrote for that public radio story, "Gone from the Carmichael's woods is a canopy of gigantic winter oaks, pecan trees, and huckleberries. Fallen limbs are everywhere. But amazing things are happening as a result. Decades-old trees that were stunted because they never saw much sun are now growing like crazy."

When the death of a baby occurs, it is not just the parents who suffer; the entire family is thrust into the chaos of grief. The experience of struggling for another child can bring up fresh layers of grief, as well as a tangle of hopeful possibilities.

Many—but not all—couples who experience the death of a child eventually go on to adopt or give birth to more children. Friends and family may react to the news with an almost palpable sense of relief. In their minds, everything is okay now. Perhaps they imagine that the new pregnancy cancels the debt of grief.

But I've yet to talk to a mother who feels this way. Every mother I know has experienced a far more complex reality. Grief for the baby does not end with the next pregnancy. It merely assumes a new form.

Father Stephen Loposky, whose daughter Kathryn died just before she was born, says that he initially struggled to understand why his wife, Daria, continued to grieve during subsequent pregnancies, even as she rejoiced at the life growing within her. But when he took a chaplaincy course at a local hospital and learned of the effects of post-traumatic stress disorder, he was able to better understand his wife's reaction.

"I understand now that when a woman who experienced the death of her first child becomes pregnant again, she does not just experience that one pregnancy," he says. "She actually experiences two simultaneously—the one she's actually having and the pregnancy she's reliving."

After Kathryn's death, each time Daria became pregnant she longed for a girl. But she went on to give birth to three boys. Each time she found out that she was carrying a boy, her grief was compounded. Her final pregnancy was the hardest: she had low amniotic fluid, placenta previa, and severe back pain, and after she gave birth she could not stop bleeding. "It was as if God was saying through her body, 'This is enough,'" Father Stephen says. And so it was nine years after Kathryn died that Daria gave birth to a healthy baby girl. "Even when she was in the womb, we were already being healed by her presence," Father Stephen says.

Healing the Past, Moving Forward

Father Stephen and Daria have worked to help their children know Kathryn. They have taken them to Kathryn's gravesite and they have shared their memories of her with them. "We tell them that she loved church music, and we tell them about how we went to the doctor's together, and then we talk about her funeral, that it was difficult and it hurt us, but that God was with us," Father Stephen explains.

As a family, they have never shied away from talking about Kathryn, or from death in general. The children have attended every funeral at the family's parish, and they have come to some peace with the reality of death. Father Stephen chuckles as he relates that his son Nick can recite the color of every casket from every church funeral going back years. He'll say, "Dad do you remember when so and so died, and their casket was blue?"

Far from being morbid, the causal casket conversation is healthy. Nick understands that death is part of the fabric of life, it is inevitable and everywhere. Because his parents haven't tried to protect him from the sight of dead bodies and the realities of grief, they have conveyed confidence in his ability to cope. Their willingness to engage the mystery of death shows their confidence that life is still bigger.

Preparing to Conceive

If you have experienced a miscarriage, stillbirth, or the death of an infant, do not underestimate your body's response to the grief. Sometimes the enormity of what has happened can only fully be realized when you set out on that path again. Each subsequent pregnancy increases your awareness of the enormity of what has happened. Doctors often speak of physical healing that must occur after a miscarriage, but the emotional and spiritual aspects of the experience must also be considered and given their due.

Rachelle, whose son Simeon died at five months, believes that therapy before subsequent pregnancies is very useful, particularly from a counselor who specializes in bereavement or fertility issues. Rachelle feels that her own unhealed wounds made future pregnancies more difficult than they needed to be. In particular, labor was difficult. "My next labor was severely hampered by emotional pain I thought I had processed, but which had not been adequately addressed," she says.

Growing a Family

Jeanette and Steven, whose son Andrew died of meningitis, understand what it means to create life in the midst of devastation. Even as they grieved for Andrew, Jeanette and Steven began to grope toward new life. Steven became interested in international adoption and began the proceedings for the adoption of a little girl from China. That little girl, Amanda, became their daughter within the year.

And in their grief, as they sought to comfort each other, they miraculously conceived Olivia, just six weeks after Andrew's death. Jeanette and Steve were shocked that the pregnancy occurred so quickly, because with Andrew it had taken a year for them to conceive. They wondered if Andrew had somehow helped them.

The second pregnancy created a storm of emotions in Jeanette's heart. She was delighted about the idea of the new life within her, and yet she was afraid of what other people might think. She wondered if people would think she was making light of Andrew's death because she and Steven conceived so quickly. And she was a little bit suspicious of her extended family's joy over their two new daughters—she didn't want anyone to forget their firstborn.

Near the middle of her pregnancy, she wrote a letter to her family, encouraging them to keep Andrew's memory alive, no matter what happened. She wrote:

> *Understand that although we're having more children and doing our best to find happiness again, that doesn't mean that everything is right with the world. Our new children will add lots of joy, but they aren't going to wipe away pain or in any way make up for losing Andrew. They'll give us new hope and return some meaning to our lives, but they won't make the grief disappear.*

Of course we will love these girls (we already do!),
but we can't forget Andrew either, and we never will.
I don't want you to forget him either. I want you to
remember what a special little guy he was. Even though
distance kept you from spending much time with him,
I want you to remember the moments you did have
with him. I want you to cherish them. Going forward,
I hope people will feel comfortable enough to talk
about Andrew and know that it's okay. Even though
it is sad, it helps to know that people care about him
and miss him.

Like Jeanette and Steven, Jim and Everly also went on
to conceive again. The struggle for a healthy pregnancy
forced Everly to go off sleeping pills and mood-related
medications and to work to become as healthy as
possible. "I didn't want to be ravaged by chemicals,"
she says. She longed for another son, and that wish
came true when she gave birth to Dylan. Although
the pregnancy was hard on her physically—she gave
birth through her third C-section—it was good for her
emotionally because it restored something that had
been taken with Simon's death: hope.

And despite all the innocence that had been lost
through Simon's death, Everly had a strong feeling
during her pregnancy with Dylan that everything was
going to be alright. "In a way, Simon lives on through
Dylan," Everly says. From her own experience and
from speaking to other parents, she understands that

having another child does help, although each child is unique and irreplaceable. Having more children doesn't close the wound, but it can give parents and siblings something to hold on to as they move forward.

The reality of the loss of a sibling stays with a family's other children and manifests itself in all kinds of unexpected ways as the years wear on. Everly remembers one time when their older daughter, Elena, was pushing her baby brother, Dylan, in the stroller and the stroller flipped over. Elena was totally terrified, and probably overreacted to the simple but easily fixed blunder, as she had come to understand how fragile life can be.

This knowledge forced the family to live and love differently than they did before. "I realize how vulnerable I am, and that life is finite—temporary. And I know that I have to appreciate every bit of beauty in each moment," Everly says. "You've just got to grab happiness wherever you can find it."

Sibling Loyalty

Steven and Jeanette's subsequent children—they now have four—love their brother Andrew, although they've never met him. He is a full part of the family. Every year on his birthday, the family bakes a cake for him and sends balloons up to heaven for him to catch.

One time when they were driving past a cemetery, Jeanette's children began to ask where Andrew was buried. Jeanette took a deep breath and explained that he wasn't actually buried, he was cremated. "Do you remember that urn in our bedroom?" she asked them. "Andrew's ashes are there."

Jeannette's children took the news in stride, in the matter-of-fact way children have. For them, it was just more information. The urn in the bedroom is not unlike Andrew's tree in the backyard, a tree that they keep lit from Thanksgiving to New Year's. If a little bit of him could be in the backyard, and if a lot of him could be in their hearts all the time, then why couldn't his ashes be upstairs in mom and dad's bedroom?

And as Jeanette says all this, she smiles at me sadly, laughing between tears at the strangeness of it all. "In the months right after he died, sometimes Steve and I slept with his urn on the bed between us."

Talking to Children
about the Death of Their Sibling

All parents say something similar about talking to living children about siblings that have died. They usually feel that it's essential to keep the door of conversation open, and to respond to their children's questions and emotions with calm honesty.

Rachelle, in fact, loves how both of her girls are sometimes fascinated with their brother, Simeon. They often ask about him, and when asked how many people are in their family, the kids never leave Simeon out of the count. "I have a wood box that my father-in-law made me to keep Simeon's keepsakes in. It has notes and cards of congratulations, as well as sympathy cards. I also have his tiny hospital wrist and ankle ID bands, a tape with the music we played at his delivery and baptism, and the tag from his cremation box. When the girls were much younger, they often asked to play with it."

It must have helped the girls to have something tangible to touch and see, to be able to use their hands to relate to the brother they never met. After somebody we love dies, we all need something to hold on to; and children, who live so concretely on this earth, value contact with something soft and solid as they try to make sense of what has happened.

Rachelle and her husband, Paul, like many parents, work to keep the door of communication open with their children, to let them inquire about their brother and to answer their questions as honestly as possible. "If you have other children, it's okay to talk to them about the child who died. Just remember that children can handle different amounts of information at different ages. Listen to what they are really asking and just tell them as much as they want to know," she explains.

The Loss of a Twin

The bond between twins can be particularly intense because the two developed together in the womb. Their very first impressions of life were formed together as they nudged each other and leaned on each other in sleep. Not only did they share their very first home, but they were nourished together, startled at the same noises, waited together to meet the same parents.

The daughter of my friend Irene Khouri, Christina, was a twin, but her sister died during the pregnancy. As Christina grew, Irene wondered when she should fill Christina in on her first nine months of life. But when Christina was five years old, she brought it up on her own. As Irene was driving, Christina said, "Mom, I feel like a part of me has been missing all my life."

"My heart fell to my stomach," Irene says. "Then Christina said, 'I just don't feel like things are quite right.'"

Irene took a deep breath and said, "Well, actually there were two of you. Your twin sister died before you were born."

"Really?" Christina said. "That makes sense."

Instead of tears, the revelation brought Christina a sense of relief. That feeling she'd had all her life that something was amiss was not an illusion after all. Something *was* amiss. But knowing the truth about her life helped her to put the pieces together, to understand that she wasn't imagining things after all.

"From then on, she talked about Elena as if she was part of the family—which, of course, she is," Irene says. The knowledge that her instincts were on target freed Christina to speak openly about her sister and ask questions such as, "What if I had died? What would it have been like?" And Christina is free to wonder what it will be like when she and the person who is most like her in the world are finally reunited.

Helping Children Grieve

When a firstborn child dies, subsequent siblings may grieve over him or her and wonder about their lost sibling, but the grief is entirely different than that of children who lose a younger sibling and can remember the brother or sister who died.

For these children, the grief is concrete and personal. They have learned that life is fragile, and they may be fearful and angry. The death of a sibling forces a child to see that Mom and Dad can't protect them from everything—they too could go in a heartbeat. This is a frightening realization for a person of any age, but can be especially difficult for a child who is just beginning to get their bearings in the world.

Elena Sparrow was four when her year-old brother, Simon, died. She must remember what it was like to have him coughing beside her. Both of them were sick with what initially seemed like a cold. But Simon's condition worsened, and he had to go to the hospital and never came back.

As emotional as it can be to talk about her brother, Elena has never lost the desire to do so. She continues to giggle about the funny things he did. And like parents who might imagine what their child would have looked like as they grew, she keeps looking for Simon's face in little boys around his age. When she and her mom pass a child on the street with curly hair, Elena often says something like, "I think Simon would have looked like him."

Elena's parents, Jim and Everly, remain open to these conversations, painful as they can be. They help keep Simon close, after all these years, affirming his place in the family and the mark he left on this earth.

Elena, who had been a calm and loving sister before her brother's death, struggled to make sense of what had happened after Simon died. She had explosive outbursts and became fearful. With the fresh knowledge that death can sometimes pounce without warning, she began to worry about her own life. When she found a pimple on her back or cut her finger, she imagined that she, too, was going to die. Her parents offered her—and continue to give her—a great deal of reassurance that not every ailment leads to death.

Everly and Jim have also had to reassure Elena that her brother's death was not her fault. Just as small children sometimes feel that they are to blame for their parents' divorce, Elena needed to know that she had not caused—nor could she have prevented—her younger brother's death. "The experience changed who she was," Everly says.

Everly remembers a few events that express something of what those early months were like for her daughter. On one occasion, Elena asked for ice cream, and when her mother said no, Elena—who had usually been reasonable about such things in the past—starting sobbing and screaming and running. Everly had to grab her and hold on to her with all her might while she called her husband for help. And there were a few times that Everly remembers taking Elena to the park only to have both of them leave sobbing. "Those first six months, I felt totally insane," Everly says. "I wanted to make myself a T-shirt that said, 'My son just died. Give me a hug—and a break.'"

A Path through Grief

Everly believes that the concrete work of caring for Elena after Simon's death helped keep her afloat. The nights were especially oppressive for Everly. Many nights, sleep just wouldn't come. But when the morning sun spread its shattered rays into their Chicago apartment, Everly couldn't just lay there on her bed and moan. Elena needed her to get up and make breakfast and help her off to school. She needed her mom to show her the path through grief.

And Everly needed Elena every bit as much as her daughter needed her. The night Simon died, Elena was her survival. Although Simon was officially pronounced dead around noon on a Saturday, by late Friday evening, Everly felt in her heart that Simon had died. Although Jim stayed at the hospital all night long caressing Simon, Everly left the hospital around two a.m. She drove home through a torrential downpour that flooded the streets of Chicago to be with her daughter. She crept into Elena's room, where she was sleeping peacefully. She crawled into bed and wrapped her arms around Elena. As the rain pelted the windows outside, she wondered how she would find the words to tell Elena that her brother had died.

In the weeks that followed Simon's death, when the apartment was suddenly packed with family and the grief was intense and surreal, Everly often took refuge in Elena's room. She'd nestle beside her daughter on the top bunk and stay there for hours.

"She was the only thing that kept me grounded. So I tried to lie by her side as much as possible, always stroking my fingers on her back for fear of losing her," Everly says. "I felt that as long as I was touching her, she would still be there."

As Everly looks back on the weeks and months after Simon's death, she realizes that it was her daughter who helped her stay in the realm of the tangible, at least some of the time. "Sleeping next to Elena was the only experience that felt kind of concrete. Most of the time I felt like I was going to crawl out of my skin and truly felt insane, like, 'This isn't happening to me; I must be in a nightmare.'"

Everly's own need to be close to Elena was probably just what Elena needed most as she struggled with her own anger and grief. Everly and Jim tried to spend extra time with Elena, to help her get back into a routine so that she would feel a little more normal. "We got through it just by loving her and reassuring her and letting her talk about Simon as much as she needed to," Everly says.

Everly, who says that she is basically agnostic, had hoped to find God through the experience of her son's death. After Simon died, she said to herself, "If I'm ever going to find God, it will probably be now." But she never seemed to come to that place of faith, despite her openness. "My husband believes in God," she says, "and it gives him solace." Everly didn't find God, but she did have the gift of Elena to keep her grounded.

Cheryl Haggard, whose fourth child, Maddux, died shortly after his birth, was able to bring her other children to the hospital to be with their baby brother before he died. The day that Maddux died, her children crowded into the hospital room to touch and caress their baby brother. Chase was twelve, Anna was nine, and Natalie was just five years old. They all got to hold him and be with him in his final hours.

Both after and before Maddux died, Cheryl was able to have professional photos taken of Maddux—but she regrets she did not have a photo taken with her other children and Maddux before he died. "Such a photo would have lasted for generations," she says. "The photo would have been there for my children's lifetimes. People would have asked my kids, 'What is this baby's story?' and they would have had a story to tell. This baby has a story to tell."

Cheryl believes that it is an invaluable experience for children to be present with their sibling both before and after death. When a baby dies during pregnancy or labor, it is particularly valuable for children to have this encounter, to hold the baby, if possible, as it will be their only opportunity in this world.

Cheryl says that part of her desire to share the experience of Maddux with her kids was that she didn't want them to live in fear or to be ashamed of their brother just because he had birth defects. "I wanted my children to know that Maddux was not a monster. That he was dying, but there was nothing to be afraid of."

Over the years, Cheryl and her husband, Mike, have tried to be open to conversations with their children about their brother. And while Cheryl initially tried to shield her children from her grief—this is why she did not have them at the hospital after he died—she has learned that it is okay to let them see her cry. It is their grief, too, after all. She and Mike have sought to be open about their grief, with each other, with their children, and with friends and family. And they have allowed the conversation to keep going with their kids, even when it is painful. "This will be their largest lesson," Cheryl says, "the one that will grow and shape the people they turn out to be."

Suggestions for Helping Siblings Grieve:

- If possible, give yourself time to grieve before you conceive again. If you do get pregnant before you've had a chance to process your grief, consider getting counseling, as the pregnancy and labor will stir up unresolved emotions, guilt, and fear.

- If the baby that dies has older siblings, try to include them as much as possible in all parts of your grieving process. Allow them to see, touch, and be photographed with their sibling, if possible.
- Encourage your kids to speak freely about their sibling, to ask questions, and to share memories. Your response to their questions will set the tone for the family discussions.
- When the grief is most intense, try to bring in additional caregivers to offer support to your other children. It can be difficult to give them what they need when you are grieving yourself. It is okay to ask for help for the sake of your kids!
- Don't be afraid to cry in front of your children. You can help them to understand that it is okay to cry and rage at death.
- Reassure them that the baby's death was not their fault, and that despite your great sadness about this death, they are the joy of your life. Say this over and over again, because they need to hear it.

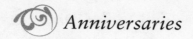 # Anniversaries

Elegy for My Son, Michael,
On the First Anniversary of His Death through
Miscarriage

I am sorry Michael.
This year has gone by and you were not in it.
Your infantile cries never stirred me in the night,
Rousing me for a diaper change or bottle.

I did not play peek-a-boo,
A thousand times around the edge of an upheld hand.
To watch you squeal with joy
At the reemergence of my face.

I never sang you to sleep,
Broken singer that I am,
Flat on my back
Feeling the sturdy weight of you against my chest.

I never stroked your soft baby hair,
Touched your baby skin, or
Like you,
Breathed a single one of your sweet baby breaths.

This year is empty
With things I never did for you.
And yet my broken heart is full,
Brimming with bitter aching love.

I am sorry Michael.
For the too short time that you were mine.
My consolation will not come until New Jerusalem
Rises from the ashes of a dead fallen world.
Then I will hold you, Michael,
And kiss you, a child
Salvaged from death,
As are we all.

—MARC SIMPSON

J recently attended a wedding with my friend Amy, whose husband died of cancer. A stranger asked where her husband was. When she told him that Jarrod died two years ago, the man said, "Oh . . ." and then, in an attempt to recover, "But you're all right now?"

"I'm approaching all right," my friend said.

I liked her honest response. She is moving toward a new kind of normal, but it is not the normal she would have imagined or wanted for herself. Later, when I asked how she felt about the man's comment, she said, "It's strange how people assume that just because time has passed everything is now okay. I feel like time is my worst enemy.

"When Jarrod first died, I thought to myself, 'Okay, I can make it a couple of weeks without him. And then a few months passed and I thought, 'okay, a few more months, I can do this.' But by the second year, the shock had worn off, and I was just left with the reality that he was really gone. As I begin to imagine all those years stretching before me without him, that's when I get really depressed."

Parents who experience the death of an infant may also be surprised by how uncontainable their grief is. It grows along with the knowledge that your child would have been walking by now, speaking, starting preschool. For many, the intensity and insanity of the first months might decrease as the years wear on, but each year, as they remember what their child might have done at this age, they feel the ache of the wound opening.

Anniversaries are particularly poignant times. Some parents will actually have a physical sensation as their bodies move into a depression around the time of the anniversary of birth or death, long before they consciously recognize why they are in such a funk. It is as if their bodies know that something has gone dreadfully wrong, and although the rest of life pushes forward, their bodies seem to be asking again and again, "What happened to me?"

Rachelle, whose baby Simeon died in the womb, described an unusual experience she had about three years after Simeon's death. She was serving as a pastor at the time and was eating lunch alone in the break room of her church. Suddenly, she felt an intense, physically painful sensation, as if she was in labor with Simeon all over again.

She didn't understand what had happened to her until she was in therapy later and learned that she had experienced a "physical memory," and that it had occurred very close to the anniversary of her son's birth. Enough time had passed and life had stabilized enough that her body had begun to process what had happened inside of it.

Because she had quickly become pregnant and given birth to more children after Simeon's death, her body had not had the chance to process what had happened. "I was finally at a point where I could begin to process things on a deeper level. I'd finally emerged out of the fog of nursing and being a brand new mom and had more space to mourn and try to understand," says Rachelle.

Dennise Kraus, who experienced two miscarriages, experiences depression each year on the anniversary of her babies' due dates. Often, she does not realize immediately why she is so blue, until she checks her calendar. Then she understands that it is like clockwork: her body still hasn't forgotten what it intended to do— birth these babies into the world. She grieves the loss of each life—and the labors that never came to pass—all over again.

Some parents develop rituals to help mark the anniversary of their child's birth or death date. Jeannette and Steven Leavitt bake a cake with their children, light candles, and sing happy birthday to Andrew, who died shortly after his first birthday.

After Candice and Steve Watters experienced the death of their son Griffin through miscarriage, they realized they needed to do something tangible to commemorate him, something that would grow and serve as a visible reminder of him, year after year. "It wasn't enough to weep," Candice says. "I needed to get out of the house and do something about the pain I was feeling. At the end of that first day we went to a tree farm, bought three apple trees and planted them on the hill in our backyard. Not only do the trees remind us of our baby, they do so with beauty and variety. They're especially sweet in the spring when the branches come alive with pink and white blossoms. We named them Griffin's Grove in honor of the baby we had planned to name Griffin George."

At that time, they also asked a couple to be Griffin's godparents, and the couple joined with Candice and Steve for the dedication of the grove on an October day. "We huddled together and shivered in the thirty-degree cold; perfect weather for bulb planting. Everyone took turns burying a promise of new life."

Candice also created a baby book for Griffin and wrote letters to him as she grieved and worked through her feelings about his death. A year after she wrote about the dedication, she wrote these words to Griffin:

> *It's so hard to believe that a whole year has passed since your due date—you would have been 1 today! It would have been your first taste of chocolate. Do they have chocolate in heaven?*
>
> *The good and really special news is that you have a baby sister now—Zoe Kathleen. She's just two weeks old. So today is bittersweet. I miss you deeply still.*

And I am overwhelmed by the joy of new life. That's what Zoe's name means. . . . We planted more bulbs in your grove—we're anticipating a spring full of life.

Even simple things, such as the first snow of winter, the first buds of spring, or a child dressed in the Halloween costume their baby was going to wear, can send parents spiraling into depression. The news of the death of another infant—even a child they did not know—can provoke a torrent of tears as their hearts break again, for their child that died prematurely—and for every child that has died too soon.

"Expect to cry a lot and at unexpected times, even for no good reason, long after you think you are over it," Juliana, mother of Philip, says. "There were several times in the summer during the height of our renovations where I just came unglued over stupid stuff like the kitchen sink being the wrong color and wailed for literally hours. You never really get over the loss of a child, but at some point your life does resume. So in the midst of the dark days, remember that it will get better someday."

Moments of intense grief come without warning and sometimes for no apparent reason, "I had a weird moment the other day walking to the library of campus, where all of a sudden I felt like my chest had been ripped open again and I was hemorrhaging grief. It passed pretty quickly, but I felt queer the rest of the day," Juliana explains.

Where Was God?

My six-year-old daughter recently drew a picture of "Jesus Calming the Storm." In her drawing, you can see a boat with several people sitting up. There are huge blue waves washing over the helm. As I studied her drawing, I was a bit mystified by the figure prone at the helm, a stick-figure man assuming a corpse-like pose, with a bolt of lightning coming down inches from his face.

"Who is that?" I asked Anna. "That's Jesus," she said, "sleeping." I loved the image so much because it captured a painful reality in a humorous way. Sometimes, even for those who believe in God, it looks like he's asleep. It looks like he is sleeping at the helm, soggy from the waves washing over the sides of the boat. The boat is about to capsize, lightning singes his hair, and still, Jesus doesn't seem to wake up.

For all of the parents I know that have lost a child, I feel like I need to try to answer the question, "Where was God?" But I can't answer it in any complete way. Instead, I will lean on the wisdom of my friend Julia Wickes, a mother herself, who reflected on this question as she prepared for a baby shower for a friend who was soon to give birth to a healthy child, even as she grieved for another friend who was preparing to birth a child who had died in the womb. She wrote to her friend:

> While at the shower, I was happy for Sarah and felt the anticipation of her little boy's arrival, sure to be tall,

smart, resourceful, capable and good looking like his parents. Another part of me, underneath, was thinking about the mother who would labor to give birth to her stillborn child that evening. It was strange to be thinking about both, and strange to live in a world that manages to contain both within its parameters.

I felt strongly that if there is a God, it can only be the God of both. Shortly after September 11, 2001, I read something that I think about often—a specific phrase. Fr. Thomas Hopko was answering the question: Where was God on September 11? He said that God was in the airplane with all the people who went down; God was in the stairwell of the collapsing towers, with the people who were trying to get out.

Everyone at the baby shower joined in a prayer for Sarah and her baby at the shower today, so I hope that God was at the baby shower—the God who adorns the whole earth with flowers. I think that God was also in the womb with the baby whose heart stopped beating last week, the God who is crowned with thorns.

This is the God I believe in: one who never forgets, who never stops loving, who is not afraid to enter imploding buildings and falling planes just to be a little closer to us. God is in the delivery room, in the stairwell, in the tomb, and in the womb. God is the one who holds every memory of every child tightly, tenderly against the backdrop of eternity.

Acknowledgments

I am deeply indebted to the parents who shared their stories. Without your courage and candor, this book would not exist. I considered changing their names and those of their babies to protect their privacy, but every parent I asked said the same thing: they wanted real names to be used. As the author of *Naming the Child*, how could I do anything less?

I would like to thank my editor, Jon Sweeney, for his enthusiasm and vision from the beginning. He's helped shape this book into something that I'm not afraid to put my own name on. And thank you to Ser Jackson, the first person to read this manuscript, for her insights, skill, and friendship.

I'm also grateful for the tireless efforts of the copyeditor, Sarah McBride, who has a great eye for detail, and for Sister Mercy Minor who helped guide the book through the final stages of publication.

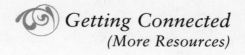 # Getting Connected
(More Resources)

Organizations

LA BELLE DAME:
JEWELRY TO NURTURE AND SUPPORT THE SPIRIT

Infant memorial jewelry and cards created by artist Kimberly de Montbrun. These pieces are lovely and reasonably priced and could be a great gift for a bereaved mother, grandmother, or aunt. Kimberly is also available to discuss custom pieces and unique ideas.

> La Bell Dame:
> Jewelry to Nurture and Support the Spirit
> 2476 TransCanada Highway
> Flat River, PEI COA 1B0
> CANADA
> 902-659-2331 ext. 1
> kimberly@labelledame.com
> www.labelledame.com

THE COMPASSIONATE FRIENDS
A national self-help organization providing friendship, support, and resources for parents and siblings grieving the loss of a child.

> The Compassionate Friends
> National Office
> P.O. Box 3696
> Oak Brook, IL 60522-3696
> 630-990-0010
> www.compassionatefriends.org

M.I.S.S.
(MOTHERS IN SUPPORT AND SOLIDARITY) FOUNDATION

An international resource providing support through online support groups, volunteer opportunities, legislative education, educational programs to reduce infant and toddler deaths, as well as information about the kindness project and an online bookstore.

> M.I.S.S.
> P.O. Box 5333
> Peoria, AZ 85385
> 623-979-1000 (local and international)
> 1.888.455.MISS (Toll free US)
> www.missfoundation.org

NOW I LAY ME DOWN TO SLEEP
—INFANT BEREAVEMENT PHOTOGRAPHY

A network of more than five thousand professional photographers located in nineteen countries who will help you remember the beauty of your baby by coming to the hospital or hospice immediately after your baby's death for a sensitive, private session. Afterward, images are retouched and presented to the parents on a CD or DVD. All services are offered free of charge.

> Now I Lay Me Down to Sleep
> —Infant Bereavement Photograpy
> Headquarters
> 7800 S. Elati St. #111
> Littleton, CO 80120
> 877-834-5667
> headquarters@nilmdts.org
> www.nowilaymedowntosleep.org

SHARE PREGNANCY AND INFANT LOSS SUPPORT, INC.

The mission of Share Pregnancy and Infant Loss Support, Inc. is to serve those whose lives are touched by the tragic death of a baby through early pregnancy loss, stillbirth, or in the first few months of life.

> Share Pregnancy and Infant Loss Support, Inc.
> National Share Office
> 402 Jackson
> St. Charles, MO 63301
> 1-800-821-6819
> share@nationalshareoffice.com
> www.nationalshareoffice.com

Books

Cacciatore, Joanne. *Dear Cheyenne*. Peoria, AZ: M.I.S.S. Foundation, 2002.

   A heartbreaking, hope-filled collection of letters and poetry that Joanne wrote for her daughter, Cheyenne, who died during labor.

Davis, Deborah L. *Empty Cradle, Broken Heart: Surviving the Death of Your Baby*. Golden, CO: Fulcrum, 1996.

   Includes practical information about the emotional, physical, and spiritual process of recovery, as well as help for navigating end-of-life decisions, planning a memorial, and caring for surviving children and those to come.

Hull-McCormack, Jerusha. *Grieving: A Beginner's Guide*. Brewster, MA: Paraclete Press, 2006.

Kluger-Bell, Kim. *Unspeakable Losses: Healing from Miscarriage, Abortion, and Other Pregnancy Loss*. New York: HarperCollins, 1998.

A self-help book for those who have experienced infertility, miscarriage, abortion, and stillbirth. Kluger-Bell is a psychotherapist and marriage and family therapist who draws on her extensive research with patients to bring to light the hidden grief surrounding these experiences. Includes helpful resources, including a guide for family and friends of couples grappling with reproductive crisis.

Lewis, C.S. *A Grief Observed*. New York: HarperCollins, 1996.

C.S. Lewis captures his own cyclical and surprising experience of grieving his wife's death. Lewis describes many of the universal realities of grief while offering a vivid glimpse into his own unique experience. This book is so raw that Lewis originally published it under a pen name, but decided to go public after friends recommended the book to him as a helpful resource.

McCracken, Anne, and Mary Semel, ed. *A Broken Heart Still Beats: After Your Child Dies*. Center City, MN: Hazelden, 1998.

A collection of poetry and quotes by bereaved parents, many of them well-known authors. This is an excellent resource for parents who feel isolated after the death of their child.

Nouwen, Henri. *Our Greatest Gift: A Meditation on Dying and Caring*. New York: HarperCollins, 1994.

A luminous book about how to better care for the dying as well as how to face your own mortality. Helpful for any person who is grappling with issues surrounding the mortality of a loved one.

DVDs

Wangerin Jr., Walter. *Confronting Death: A Christian Approach to End of Life with Walter Wangerin*. Brewster, MA: Paraclete Press, 2008.

Notes

12 *It's hard to live among normal people now.* "Man with a Mission," *Time* vol. 135 no. 15 (April 9, 1990), available online at http://www.time.com/time/magazine/article/0,9171,969787,00.html.

13 *Nobody knew you* Jan Cosby, "Nobody Knew You," *Mothering* (July/August 2002), p. 57. Used with permission of the author.

18 *I had the same feeling about my son,* Martha Beck, *Expecting Adam* (New York: Penguin, 1999), pp. 156–157.

24 *An odd by product of my loss* C.S. Lewis, *A Grief Observed* (New York: HarperCollins, 1996), pp. 10–11.

30 *You will give birth to her soon,* Claudia Mair Burney, "For Twinnie," July 16, 2004. Available online at http://ragamuffindiva.blogspot.com. Used with permission of the author.

32 *He was very tiny, about the length of my arm* Rachelle Mee-Chapman, "Dia de los Muertos," November 2, 2007. Online at http://www.magpie-girl.com.

34 *"Look, John, it's not as though* Beck, *Expecting Adam,* p. 132.

34 *"This is the story of two driven Harvard academics* Ibid, p. 7.

42 *"new road before me and a new meaning in life,* From an article by Jim Forest, published online at http://www.incommunion.org. Much of this essay was originally published in Jim Forest's

introduction to *Mother Maria Skobtsova: Essential Writings* (Maryknoll, NY: Orbis Books, 2003).

43   *You can ask why, but don't be surprised*   Burney, "For Twinnie." http://ragamuffindiva.blogspot.com/2004/07/for-twinnie.html. Used with permission of the author.

45   *I looked at your perfect, lifeless body.*   Joanne Cacciatore, *Dear Cheyenne* (Peoria, AZ: M.I.S.S. Foundation, 2002), p. 9. ©1999, 2007 All Rights Reserved. Used with permission of the author.

52   *"The secret is that the flyer does nothing*   Henri Nouwen, *Our Greatest Gift: A Meditation on Dying and Caring* (New York: HarperCollins, 1994), p. 15.

53   *"Don't be afraid. Remember*   Ibid.

55   *With an anxious and hurried look,*   Anton Pavlovich Chekhov, "Grief," in *The Stories of Anton Chekhov,* tr. Robert N. Linscott (New York: The Modern Library, 1959), p. 107.

60   *When she spoke for any length of time*   Maeve Brennan, "The Eldest Child," *The New Yorker,* June 29, 1968, p. 30.

60   *"There is a time simply to be present*   Richard John Neuhaus, "Born Toward Dying," *First Things* 100 (February 2000): 15–22.

62   *"It is hard to have patience*   Lewis, *A Grief Observed,* p. 15.

65   *The worst thing is not the sorrow*   Neuhaus, "Born Toward Dying."

65   *"He will never 'get over it,'"*   Lewis, *A Grief Observed,* p. 52.

68   *Yours was the heart*   Daniel Ladinsky, "Yours Was the Heart," original poem for this book, previously unpublished. Used with permission.

78   *The memory of my own response*   John Tittensor, *Year One: A Record* (New York: Penguin, 1987), as quoted in *A Broken Heart Still Beats: After Your Child Dies* by Anne McCracken and Mary Semel, (Center City, MN: Hazelden Publishing, 1998), p. 211.

90   *At first my father tried to*   Ursula Hegi, *Floating in My Mother's Palm* (New York: Vintage Books, 1991), p. 96.

90   *"Where you end up*   Lynn Darling, "For Better or For Worse," *Esquire*, May 1996, as quoted in *A Broken Heart Still Beats: After Your Child Dies* by Anne McCracken and Mary Semel, (Center City, MN: Hazelden Publishing, 1998).

91   *My husband and I would never*   Ibid. p.105.

91   *Recent studies suggest that about one in four couples*   This study was conducted in 2006 by Directions Research, Inc. for the Compassionate Friends, Inc.

103   *Enter each day with the expectation*   Sam Keen, *Hymns to the Unknown God: Awakening the Spirit in Everyday Life* (New York: Bantam Books, 1995), p. 281.

114   *"Thinking my imagination had gone wild,* Cacciatore, *Dear Cheyenne,* p. 21.

114   *I wake each morning*   Anne Morrow Lindbergh, *Hour of Gold, Hour of Lead, Diaries and Letters of Anne Morrow Lindbergh 1929–1932* (New York: Harcourt Brace & Company, 1973), p. 27.

118   *The intuitive mind*   Albert Einstein, *Cosmic Religion, with Other Opinions and Aphorisms* (New York: Corici-Friede, 1931).

118   *the study was complete and released to his academic colleagues.*   The quotations from Dr. Shamas are taken from a personal e-mail correspondence with the author.

124   *"The silent voice that had alerted me to the danger* Beck, *Expecting Adam,* pp. 155–156

127   *Why can't they understand?*   Cacciatore, *Dear Cheyenne,* p. 64.

145   *Elegy for My Son, Michael,*   Marc Simpson, "Elegy for My Son Michael on the First Anniversary of His Death through Miscarriage," originally published on Orthodox Circle, http:// orthodoxcircle.com. Used with permission of the author.

149   *"It wasn't enough to weep,"*   Candice Watters, "I Never Knew You, Still I Love You," published on Focus on the Family website, http://family.org/ lifechallenges/A000000814.cfm.

149   *It's so hard to believe*   Ibid.

151   *While at the shower,*   Julia Wickes, "God in the Stairwell,"   http://flakedoves.blogspot.com (December 1, 2007). Used with permission of the author.

About Paraclete Press

Who We Are

Paraclete Press is a publisher of books, recordings, and DVDs on Christian spirituality. Our publishing represents a full expression of Christian belief and practice—from Catholic to Evangelical, from Protestant to Orthodox.

We are the publishing arm of the Community of Jesus, an ecumenical monastic community in the Benedictine tradition. As such, we are uniquely positioned in the marketplace without connection to a large corporation and with informal relationships to many branches and denominations of faith.

What We Are Doing

BOOKS | Paraclete publishes books that show the richness and depth of what it means to be Christian. Although Benedictine spirituality is at the heart of all that we do, we publish books that reflect the Christian experience across many cultures, time periods, and houses of worship. We publish books that nourish the vibrant life of the church and its people— books about spiritual practice, formation, history, ideas, and customs.

We have several different series, including the best-selling Living Library, Paraclete Essentials, and Paraclete Giants series of classic texts in contemporary English; A Voice from the Monastery—men and women monastics writing about living a spiritual life today; award-winning literary faith fiction and poetry; and the Active Prayer Series that brings creativity and liveliness to any life of prayer.

RECORDINGS | From Gregorian chant to contempor-ary American choral works, our music recordings celebrate sacred choral music through the centuries. Paraclete distributes the recordings of the internationally acclaimed choir Gloriæ Dei Cantores, praised for their "rapt and fathomless spiritual intensity" by American Record Guide, and the Gloriæ Dei Cantores Schola, which specializes in the study and performance of Gregorian chant. Paraclete is also the exclusive North American distributor of the recordings of the Monastic Choir of St. Peter's Abbey in Solesmes, France, long considered to be a leading authority on Gregorian chant.

DVDs | Our DVDs offer spiritual help, healing, and biblical guidance for life issues: grief and loss, marriage, forgiveness, anger management, facing death, and spiritual formation.

LEARN MORE ABOUT US AT OUR WEB SITE:
www.paracletepress.com
or call us toll-free at 1-800-451-5006.

You may also be interested in...

Grieving: A Beginner's Guide

ISBN: 978-1-55725-493-1
Paperback, $14.95

"This book is designed to help those in pain—and specifically those who have lost someone through death—to imagine the path before them. It is a path of suffering. But it is also a path that may lead to unexpected discoveries—and to peace."—Jerusha McCormack

"This book is a personal, concrete exploration of ways to deal with the pain of loss. It is a book of lessons learned first-hand by the author in her own grieving, and so the book has an unusual immediacy and usefulness. I can imagine giving it to friends as a first resource."
—Thomas Moore, author of *The Care of the Soul*

"McCormack writes straight from the heart in simple language that is infused with a spirituality that is never preachy or pushy. . . . Anyone who is grieving or anyone who knows a grieving person will find hope and support in this small book."—*Publishers Weekly*, starred review

Available from Paraclete Press
www.paracletepress.com
1-800-451-5006

You may also be interested in...

At a Loss for Words

*How to Help Those You Care for
in a Miscarriage, Stillbirth,
or Newborn Death Experience*

ISBN: 978-1-55725-386-6
$29.95, DVD

When a miscarriage, stillbirth, or newborn death occurs, many of us want to reach out, but feel unsure of what to say and do. *At a Loss for Words* teaches family members, friends, neighbors, and early caregivers—clergy, doctors, and counselors—how to help.